SECRET
LEWES

Terry Philpot

AMBERLEY

About the Author

Terry Philpot has written and edited twenty books including *31 London Cemeteries to Visit Before You Die* (2012) and *Beside the Seaside: Brighton's Places and Its People* (2015). He has contributed nineteen entries to the *Oxford Dictionary of National Biography*. He writes regularly for *The Tablet* and has written for a wide range of publications including *The Guardian* and *The Independent*.

For Sally Sharp and John Pierson, who, I am sure, know all about this.

First published 2017

Amberley Publishing
The Hill, Stroud
Gloucestershire, GL5 4EP

www.amberley-books.com

Copyright © Terry Philpot, 2017
Copyright © Photographers, as attributed, 2017

The right of Terry Philpot to be identified as the Author of this work has been asserted in accordance with the Copyrights, Designs and Patents Act 1988.

ISBN 978 1 4456 6196 4 (print)
ISBN 978 1 4456 6197 1 (ebook)

British Library Cataloguing in Publication Data.
A catalogue record for this book is available from the British Library.

Origination by Amberley Publishing.
Printed in Great Britain.

Contents

Preface

The reader who picks up a book titled *Secret Lewes* has the right to ask what can there be secret about so ancient a town, about which much is known already? There is much that is very obvious – the castle, the priority ruins, some outstanding buildings, the twittens, and so on – but to see them only stimulates imagination and interest. From these flow questions such as 'how old is that building?' 'Who built it?' and 'Who lived there?' A secret is that which is not known by the majority, but there are also unknown stories and information about otherwise well-known, even famous places, people and events.

All such secrets of the buildings and the people, some buried (often literally) beneath 1,500 years of history, are uncovered in this book.

Terry Philpot
October, 2016

1. A Concise History of Lewes

School Hill and Lewes High Street

Lewes may take its name from the Celtic word meaning slope or the Saxon word *hluews* or *hlaew*, meaning mound or hill. This is exemplified by its topography and harks back to the first significant period of settlement in the town's important history.

There are 3,000-year-old burial mounds at Landport Bottom and there may have been a primitive iron industry in Lewes 2,500 years ago. There were pre-Roman hill forts too, set around what we now call Lewes, and all of this was set in the gentle, fertile farming land. The hill forts did not survive invasion but mounds and ditches are evidence of what existed before the Saxons. But there were no notable settlements in Roman and pre-Roman times. The Romans came in the first century AD, for the River Ouse afforded a suitable landing point for the invaders. Archeological digs have thrown up evidence of Roman road building and items or fragments of pottery, coins and jewellery.

The Saxons probably founded the town in the sixth century, 100 or so years after their invasion of East Sussex. The present medieval street pattern of the High Street dates from the period between the Saxons to the 1500s, but to the Saxons it owes one of its most pleasing features, the twittens – the pathways cut through, falling down from where the castle now stands in the north to the south.

Alfred had created a fortified network of burhs, or fortified settlements, across his kingdom in the latter part of the ninth century and by the early tenth century Lewes was made a burh. The *Burghal Hideage*, compiled at the time of Edward the Elder (899–924), king of Wessex, gives the first written mention of Lewes, which is said to be the eleventh largest of the thirty-three burhs. These were made to repel an attack from the Danes, in which event the men of Lewes were called to fight. A ditch, with an earth rampart, with probably an earth stockade on top, surrounded the town in those days, and it is likely that in the last third of the eleventh century this had been replaced by a wall around the town. None remain today but the suffix 'gate', as in many towns and cities, signifies where the entry points would have been. However, while Lewes' geographical position was to make it vulnerable to the Norman invader, at this time its physical surroundings gave it shelter from any real threat from the north.

Lewes prospered. There were weekly markets and by the tenth century there were two mints. However, by the time the Normans arrived in 1066, the population was probably no more than 2,000. Lewes gained a charter in 1148, whereby some rights were given to the townspeople, and the Middle Ages saw its emergence as a port, with grain and wool exports.

Lewes was given as a gift to William de Warenne and his wife Gundrada (often mistakenly said to be William the Conqueror's daughter), but her husband had fought with the king and acquired the earldom of Sussex. He built a wooden castle here, which stands now rebuilt in stone. But there was a sorrier end for the other structure that William

Left and below: The gate of the
Franciscan Greyfriars Friary in Friary
Walk, with its plaque, although it was
removed from its original location.
(Terry Philpot)

THE ONLY SURVIVING PART OF THE
GREYFRIARS FRANCISCAN FRIARY
ONCE BY THE JUNCTION OF FRIARS WALK
AND THE HIGH STREET. BUILT IN 1224,
DEMOLISHED AS PART OF THE DISSOLUTION
IN 1538, THEN RE-ERECTED HERE
IN THE MIDDLE OF
THE 19TH CENTURY.

and Gundrada gave to the town. Thanks to the Dissolution of the Monasteries, the Priory of St Pancras, the first Cluniac priory in England, stands now in picturesque ruins.

The priory was only one of a number of monastic foundations in the town. The Franciscans arrived in the thirteenth century but only a gate of Greyfrairs Friary remains (next to the Quaker Meeting House in Friary Walk), and even that is not in its original position. As if Thomas Cromwell's depredations were not enough, the town was struck by plague (not the only time) in 1538, a year after the priory's destruction.

The Dissolution of the Monasteries was the second of the three great events in Lewes' history. The first had taken place 300 years earlier with the Battle of Lewes, when Simon de Montfort and his rebellious nobles defeated and captured his brother-in-law Henry III.

The battle is the most significant of Lewes' events because it was the climax of the Second Barons' War, Britain's unknown civil war. This was provoked by royal autocracy, favouritism at court, foreign policy and a refusal to negotiate with the barons. Henry was attempting to evade the Provisions of Oxford, whereby a baronial council, chaired by de Montfort, was to meet three times a year to discuss administration and inheritance laws.

By the time Henry reached Lewes, in the hope of rest and reinforcement, the conflict with de Montfort had proved a bloody one.

When Henry rejected de Montfort's peace proposals, the rebels attacked from Offham Hill on 14 May 1264. Though greatly outnumbered, de Montfort routed the Royalist forces within hours. The battle was a disaster for Henry. The fighting was fierce: 2,700 men lost their lives, and the town burned as de Montfort's troops advanced.

Part of the site of the Battle of Lewes, as seen today from Castle Precincts. (Paul Lantsbury)

The bronze helmet on a concrete base, unveiled in 1964 at Lewes Priory Gardens to commemorate the 700th anniversary of the Battle of Lewes. (Terry Philpot)

It is uncertain exactly where between the top of Offham Hill and the medieval town the battle was fought. Lewes has spread beyond its medieval boundaries, but today some, at least, of the battlefield can be observed from the viewing place in Castle Precincts, on the left up from the bowling green, where school playing fields and houses are largely hidden by lush vegetation in the valley.

Richard of Cornwall, younger brother of the king, fled to shelter at Snellings Mill. A plaque at the spot in Western Road, at right angles to the Black Horse pub, tells us, 'Richard, thah [though] thou be ever trichard [traitor], trichen [betray] shalt thou never more.' Henry took refuge in the priory but finally surrendered.

The Mise of Lewes, the agreement that followed the battle, diminished royal power and is seen as the indirect path to present-day parliamentary democracy.

The third historic event for which Lewes is known came from the attempt by Mary Tudor, daughter of Henry VIII, to reimpose Catholicism. The five years of her reign (1553–58) led to more than 280 Protestants being put to death, many of them meeting the same fate as seventeen who died in Lewes, outside what was then the Star Inn and is now the Town Hall, in the High Street – they were burned at the stake.

These events did not stay the town's prosperity, and it was a port centuries before Brighton emerged from fishing villages as a rival in the first third of the nineteenth century. For centuries, Lewes had been the administrative and judicial centre of Sussex

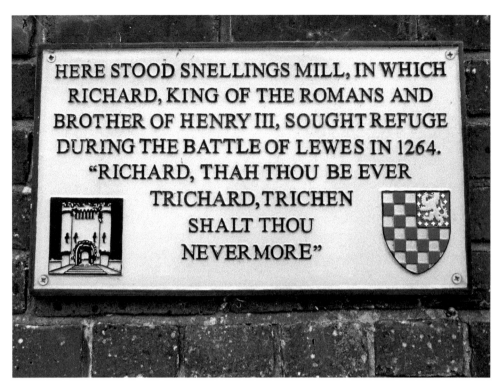

The plaque in Western Road, the site of Snellings Mill, to mark where Richard, brother of Henry III, took refuge during the Battle of Lewes. (Terry Philpot)

and was incorporated as a borough in 1881. When East Sussex came into being in 1888 it was the county town, although the Town Hall (now home to the town council) was not built until 1893.

The creation of the Improvement Commissioners in 1806 saw the town's streets paved and cleaned. There was gas lighting in 1822 and electricity in 1901. The opening of the railway in 1846 increased its attraction as a place to live and as a commercial centre, but this spelled the end of Lewes as a port. The station was situated in Friars Walk, and closed in 1857 when a junction station was built just north of the present station, which was built in 1889.

Industry flourished and the foundries expanded, but Lewes' population growth has been slower than one might expect. It was 1,500 in the last part of the thirteenth century and by 1901 it was 11,000. In 2001 it had reached 15,988 and ten years later it was 17,297.

As in all towns and cities, there has been suburban growth and places like South Malling, Cliffe and Landport, once distinct villages, have been subsumed within 'greater' Lewes. But its character has not been lost and even a Saxon looking at the map of his time and one of today would recognise the basic pattern of the town, while later residents, who'd be surprised by the car, would not think themselves in a wholly unknown place.

2. Exactly the Right Places

Twittens

Residents and visitors may be shopping, visiting or just looking at some of Lewes' attractive and often ancient buildings. And while they will traverse the rise of School Hill and the High Street, or dip down to the Cliffe Bridge, they will surely walk along the twittens.

The earliest meaning of 'twitten' is a narrow path between two walls or hedges, especially on hills. But as hamlets grew into villages and villages into towns, twitten has come to mean small passageways between (sometimes) buildings leading to courtyards, streets, or open areas.

Today, they are a grid of narrow, cobbled alleys that date from Saxon and Norman times. They are ancient passageways, some fronted by later houses and usually with flint or stone walls. (Alleys and passageways elsewhere in the country have similar origins but they are known by other names). Our ancestors would have walked along these same paths a thousand years or more ago.

Castle Lane. (Paul Lantsbury)

Brooman's Lane. (Terry Philpot)

Green Lane. (Terry Philpot)

Paine's Twitten. (Terry Philpot)

Twittens are usually at right angles to the main highway and while most are, many south of the High Street, dating from Saxon times, are not.

The use of the word twitten appears to date from the thirteenth century and may relate to 'twiete', an early German word meaning a narrow lane or alleyway. The word is also said to derive from 'betwixt and between'.

We have lost Old Scole Strete and Pinwell Street, while Fuller Passage is now a nondescript cul-de-sac of small businesses, and St Mary's Lane is unrecognisable as Station Street. But particularly attractive are Green Lane, Brooman's Lane, Church Lane, Paines Twitten, Watergate Lane, and St Andrew's Lane.

Two twittens deserve special mention:

Pipe Passage

Pipe Passage may well have been the sentry walk along the castle wall. It is named for the clay-pipe kiln laid here in the eighteenth and early nineteenth centuries. Over the years its name has chopped and changed: Pipe Alley and Clock Alley (both 1826); Pipes Passage (1860, with the 's' lost in 1938); Western Terrace (1871 and again in 1921 and 1927); and Western Passage (1891). To walk along here is to walk where those who protected Saxon and Norman Lewes stood on watch. It also contains the remains of one of the ancient windmills that once surrounded the town, whose smock (tower), the sweeps (sails) and the workings were removed in 1819. It is now the quaint brick- and flint-built Round House. It was once, for a short while, owned but not inhabited by Virginia Woolf.

Pipe Passage.
(Paul Lantsbury)

Keere Street

This is one of the most attractive of Lewes' streets (let alone of its twittens), although its steep, medieval blue-cobbled surface has all but gone, mostly replaced by the more common brown cobbling. While cobbles paved most of Lewes' streets, Keere is one of the very few remaining where the cobbling is extensive.

Keere Street likely existed before the Conquest. The name may come from the Old English *caer*, meaning a street in the fosse or ditch of the town wall. But the Saxon *cerre*, meaning sloping or winding, could also account for the name. A deed of 1272 refers to 'a path called Kerestrete'.

DID YOU KNOW?

Tradition has it that it was in Keere Street in the late eighteenth century that the Prince Regent, later George IV, drove his coach and horses recklessly down the street for a bet. He was driving from a meeting at the Lewes racecourse to dine at Southover Grange at the foot of the street.

In 1799 a local paper said that he rode on through the town to the top of School Hill, dismounted and led his horse to the bottom, which would have been kinder on the horse than a charge down cobbled Keere Street.

Keere Street.
(Terry Philpot)

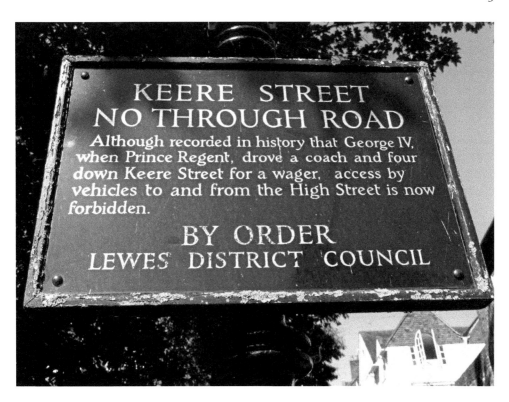

Above: George IV sign on Keere Street.
(Terry Philpot)

Right: The site of what is now
St Michael's Court was given for the
benefit of the poor of the parish of
St Michaels-in-Lewes in 1688.
(Terry Philpot)

It was called Care Hill or Scare Street in 1774. A guinea was paid to one resident, along with a shilling 'to wash James Kent of the smallpox', and for 'watching the smallpox' on Scare Street (presumably to alert others of any further outbreak).

St Michael's Court has a plaque which tells us that in 1688 Thomas Matthew, a Presbyterian woollen draper in the High Street, gave his house on this site for the benefit of the poor in the parish of St Michaels-in-Lewes. In 1858 it was decided that the present building would be used to house 'six deserving poor widows or poor single women not less than fifty years of age'. The almshouses closed in 1960.

Lewes Castle

The castle, one of the oldest Norman castles in the country, began as a wooden keep. It is a fine example of a motte-and-bailey castle, but, unusually, with two mottes (Lincoln is the only other such example). It was begun in 1069 by William de Warenne, who later founded the Priory of St Pancras and is known to have fought with William I on the field at battle. Over the next 300 years it was added to, with the magnificent Barbican Gate added in the early fourteenth century.

Today, the castle, in a fine state of preservation, remains Lewes' highest point – a steep walk to the top and the adjacent keep affords spectacular views – and towers above today's Lewes as de Warenne intended.

Mileage marker on the shopfront of the Fifteenth Century Bookshop. (Terry Philpot)

The Barbican Gate and Lewes Castle.
(Paul Lantsbury)

Anne of Cleves House

This timber-framed Wealden house, at No. 52 Southover High Street, dates from the fifteenth century, with additions up to 300 years later. It was given to Anne of Cleves as part of the manor of Southover, which came to her in her amicable annulment settlement with Henry VIII in 1540. However, atmospheric though it is, with its authentically furnished rooms, Anne never lived here, but she did rent it out. The stone carvings along the corridor are from the priory ruins. A barrel-vaulted cellar below the main hall is thought to predate the present house and is possibly dates from the fourteenth century.

The pretty enclosed gardens are inspired by Tudor planting and contain a medlar tree.

Now a museum run by the Sussex Archeological Society, the house also contains the Museum of Lewes History, and material on Tom Paine and the Wealden iron industry.

The Fifteenth-Century Bookshop

In days when bookshops seem to close as rapidly as pubs, Lewes is fortunate to retain those it does. The bookshop at Nos 99–100 High Street is an excellently preserved 600-year-old beam-framed house. In the eighteenth century tobacco pipes were made here. Above street level at the front is an old milestone giving 8 miles as the distance to Brighthelmston, a name for Brighton that fell out of use in the early 1800s. For good measure, the marker also informs the traveller that Lewes is 50 miles from Westminster Bridge and 49 miles from The Standard in Cornhill in the City of London.

The Fifteenth Century Bookshop. (Paul Lantsbury)

Sign of the former White Lion public house, Westgate Street. (Paul Lantsbury)

White Lion Sign

The White Lion, which sits on a metal bracket in Westgate Street, once graced the public house that was built in White Lion Lane in 1832. It was demolished in 1939, and the Friends of Lewes rescued the sign. There is evidence, however, of another inn standing on the site from Elizabethan times, which gave the street its earlier name.

Mathematical Tiles

These attractive tiles have been used extensively in south-east England, particularly in Sussex and Kent but largely in Lewes and Brighton, since the seventeenth century. It has been said that they came into use to avoid a tax on bricks, introduced in 1784, but their use well predates that event and, anyway, they were also taxed.

We don't know why they are so named, unless it is to do with the exactness of each tile. They have large pegs at the rear and when these are nailed onto wooden laths in overlapping layers, they resemble brickwork, as intended, set on timber-framed buildings.

Often now associated with quite expensive properties, they were a cheaper alternative to the use of ashlar stone or the rubbed brickwork required of the geometrically-composed Palladian buildings of the eighteenth century. They were manufactured in different colours, with colouring achieved either through the addition of brick dust to the raw clay, or through the use of a liquid slip. An especially remarkable example of the coloured tile is Jireh Chapel in Malling Street, which is clad in red tiles and dark-grey slate. Other

Above: Close-up of mathematical tiles. (Paul Lantsbury)

Left: Black Tile Cottage, No. 13 Western Road. (Terry Philpot)

good examples of the tiles are to be seen at No. 204 School Hill and No. 9 Market Street. Bartholomew House at Castle Gate, at the entrance to the Lewes Castle, and Black Tile Cottage, No. 13 Western Road, are both wholly clad in black tiles.

The tiles became popular in their own right and many medieval buildings were refaced with them; they offer good protection from the elements. Mathematical tiles never achieve the flat uniformity of brick but they have their own attractiveness, enhanced by how reflected light acts upon them.

The Town Hall

This attractive, red-brick building was built on the site of the Star Inn in 1893. The inn, with the Corn Exchange, had been purchased three years earlier for £4,100.

The Town Hall boasts an intricately carved, wooden, Jacobean staircase. This came to the Star Inn from the mansion of Slaugham Place, near Haywards Heath, in 1760, by then long-derelict and now existing as only as a picturesque ruin. The inn also had old panelling, which was incorporated in the new building.

Visitors can ask permission to take the steep steps down to the undercroft, used, it is said, to hold at least ten of the Protestant martyrs before they were taken outside to be burned at the stake in the mid-sixteenth century. The plaque, affixed to the wall of the Town Hall in 1949, attests to this fact with the words: 'In the vaults beneath this building were imprisoned ten of the seventeen Protestant Martyrs who were burned at the stake within a few yards of this site (1555–1557). Their names are recorded on the Memorial to be seen on Cliffe Hill. "Faithful unto Death".'

The Town Hall. (Terry Philpot)

The Jacobean staircase in the Town
Hall, formerly in the Star Inn.
(Paul Lantsbury)

Edward Reeves Photography and Harvey's Brewery

Edward Reeves Photography is believed to be the world's longest established
photographic business. The eponymous founder was a watchmaker and jeweller, who
became interested in the new art of photography and took his first portrait photograph
in 1855. In 1858 he moved to No. 159 High Street, where the company continues today.
It remains a family business, run by Edward's great-grandson Tom, the fourth generation
of Reeves' photographers.

DID YOU KNOW?

It was announced by Greene King in 2006 that it would no longer sell the local beer
Harvey's Sussex Best Bitter from the pumps of its pub the Lewes Arms, Mount Place.
There was a petition and the mayor and the local MP spoke against the decision,
and there was coverage in national newspapers and on TV and radio. With adverse
publicity and a 133-day boycott, Greene King reversed its decision in 2007. (The pub
has since changed owners and is now in the hands of Fuller, Smith and Turner.)

Harvey's Brewery. (Paul Lantsbury)

Harvey's Brewery, owned by the eighth generation of the family and founded more than 225 years ago, is the only one of Lewes' seven breweries still in existence. While most of the present building dates from 1880, the brewery has been on its riverside site since Georgian times.

Meridian Line Markers

Lewes is one of those towns through which the Greenwich Meridian runs, the line starting at the monument in Peacehaven. Lewes is unusual in having three markers to attest to the fact. A brick column was erected in Landport in 1938. There is a plaque set into the pavement in Western Road, near the junction of Spital Road. Those who visit can stand astride it with one foot in the eastern hemisphere and the other in the western. Strangely, given how many Meridian points there are in the town, the third marker is set in the wall at No. 101a Western Road, next to this pavement one and erected at the same time.

Bowling Green and Pells Pool

Lewes has a very unusual, maybe even a unique, distinction in that it contains two places of recreation said to be the oldest of their kind. The Bowling Green in Castle Precincts, up through the Barbican Gate, is the oldest rough bowling green in continuous use in England and was founded in 1640. Its players, members of a society founded in 1753, use special wooden ovals, and the most famous person to play here is Tom Paine.

The other place of recreation is the Pells Pool, which is the oldest documented freshwater outdoor public swimming pool in the United Kingdom, opening in 1861 and paid for by

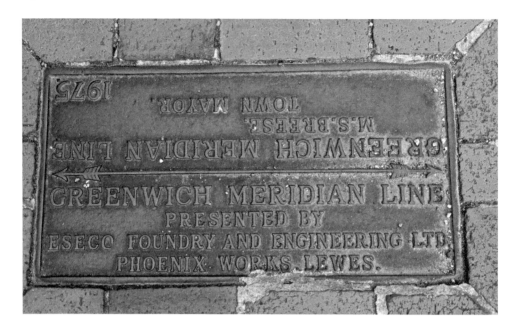

Two Meridian Line markers in Western Road, one (above) set in the pavement, the other (left) on the wall next to it. (Terry Philpot)

The bowling green, Castle Precincts. (Paul Lantsbury)

public subscription at a cost of £442.5s. The year 2011 marked its 150th anniversary and it is spring-fed. Originally there were two pools next to one another in what is properly called a lido. The land on which the pools were built was the Town Brook, given to the townspeople in 1603 by lawyer John Rowe.

3. In Character: Some Lewes People

Dr Richard Russell.

House of Dr Gidgeon Martell, High Street.
(Terry Philpot)

Dr Richard Russell

It was not the Prince Regent who first drew people to Brighton but Lewes-born physician Richard Russell, who popularised curative water treatment in the town. He was the eldest of the seven children of an apothecary and was born on 26 November 1687 in the High Street (at a house now numbered 77 and by an odd coincidence opposite the house where Gideon Mantell was later to live). His maternal grandfather was a yeoman from Southerham, near Lewes. Russell attended the town's grammar school and was probably apprenticed to a surgeon in London, training as a physician and surgeon and gaining a medical degree from the University of Leiden. He returned to England to set up a practice in his native town.

He became quickly established as the leading physician in East Sussex, soon prosperous enough to invest in property. Despite her parents' opposition, he married Mary Kempe, in South Malling, near Lewes, in December 1719.

He had observed how people living on the coast drank seawater (iodine being the key element) to cure stomach disorders, and he developed a therapeutic regime of seawater bathing and drinking, which he urged his patients to follow in Brighton, as this was judged superior to inland spas. In around 1750 in Hove, Russell created a small spa at St Anne's Wells and recommended its use to his patients.

His 1753 treatise *A Dissertation Concerning the Use of Sea Water in the Diseases of the Glands*, which he had published in Latin three years earlier, distilled his ideas. The curative effects of the water treatment were combined with diet and hygiene routines and recovery was also aided by the attraction of being in Brighton.

The next year he moved to a substantial house in Brighton that he had built, where the Royal Albion Hotel now stands. It was for use by his patients, but was also large enough to accommodate himself and his family. He lived there until 1759. He was elected a fellow of the Royal Society in 1752 and was awarded a medical degree from Cambridge University.

Russell died in 1759 and was buried at South Malling Church. The statement on Russell's commemorative tablet reads: 'If you seek his monument, look around' – this may not be original or apply to where he rests but of Brighton it is, nevertheless, very true.

Thomas Frewen

Before Edward Jenner, pioneer of the world's first smallpox vaccine, there was Thomas Frewen, a surgeon and apothecary and later a physician. He was born in Northiam, Sussex, in 1704, practised in Rye, and was later a physician in Lewes where he lived in a large Tudor house in what is now Albion Street and which had been the site of the Turk's Head Inn.

Frewen was one of the first physicians in England to adopt the practice of inoculation with smallpox. He recorded the data of around 350 patients in *The Practice and Theory of Inoculation* in 1749. Only one patient died during the process.

Frewen said that 'the common sort of people' were opposed to inoculation and 'disputed about the lawfulness of propagating diseases'. Frewen believed that animalcula, hatched from eggs and lodged in such places as the hairs and pores of human bodies, propagated smallpox and many other diseases.

In 1759, in another essay, he argued that many people who were expected to catch it escaped smallpox, and that, contrary to the views of others, medication such as aethiops mineral was irrelevant.

Frewen was eighty-six when he died at Northiam in Sussex, in 1791.

Dr Gideon Martell

Mantell was a surgeon whose first practice was in his home town of Lewes. He was born at a tall, narrow cottage at No. 23 Station Street (then St Mary's Lane) in 1790, the middle of eight children of Thomas Mantell, a shoemaker, and Sarah Austen.

Mantell's most lasting legacy is his discovery, announced in February 1825, of *Iguanodon*, one of various kinds of dinosaur (a term not adopted until 1842), after he explored the rich vertebrae deposits in the Tilgate Forest in nearby Cuckfield.

As a young man he had developed geological interests (the first of his twelve books, published in 1822, was *The Fossils of the South Downs*). In the countryside around Lewes, Mantell foraged in the pits and quarries, discovering the shells of sea urchins, ammonites, fish bones, coral, and the remains of dead animals.

Young Gideon and his siblings were barred from attending local grammar schools, which were reserved for the children of Anglicans, as their father was a Methodist (a fact that also precluded a university education). Thus, he attended a dame school in the same street as the family home, where an aged woman taught him basic reading and writing. When she died, his teaching passed to John Button, whose Whig opinions were shared by Mantell senior. After two years of his tutoring, Mantell was sent to Wiltshire for private study in the care of his uncle, a Baptist minister.

Home of Dr Richard Russell, No. 166 High Street. (Terry Philpot)

Birthplace of Dr Gideon
Martell, No. 23 Station Street.
(Terry Philpot)

When, at the age of fifteen, Mantell came back to Lewes, a local Whig leader helped him get an apprenticeship with James Moore, a surgeon of Castle Place. He served a five-year apprenticeship with Moore, with his food and lodging taken care of by his master. His early tasks included separating and arranging drugs and cleaning vials, but he graduated to the level of being able to make pills and other pharmaceutical products. He delivered medicines, kept the practice accounts, wrote out bills and extracted teeth from his patients.

When his father died in July 1807 and left his son money to pursue his studies, Mantell began to think of a medical education. Teaching himself human anatomy, he then went to London to begin a formal medical education and in 1811 became a member of the Royal College of Surgeons, and was also authorised to take on midwifery. Returning to Lewes, he went into partnership with James Moore, once his master. He was active in the outbreak of cholera, typhoid and smallpox epidemics, attended fifty patients a day and delivered between 200 and 300 babies a year. The practice's profits rose by £250 to £750 a year.

Although mainly occupied with his busy medical practice, he spent his little free time pursuing his passion, geology, often working into the early hours of the morning, identifying fossil specimens he found at the marl pits in Hamsey, 5 miles north of Lewes.

His correspondence in 1813 with James Sowerby, naturalist and illustrator, caused the latter to name one of the species *Ammonites mantelli*. That year Mantell was elected as a fellow of the Linnaean Society of London and two years later he published his first paper on the characteristics of the fossils found in the Lewes area.

He married twenty-year-old Ann Woodhouse, daughter of one of his deceased patients, at St Marylebone Church, London, in 1816. They lived in Lewes at what is now No. 166 High Street and she would come to provide lithographs for his books. That same year he purchased the medical practice from Moore and took up an appointment at the Royal Artillery Hospital, at Ringmer, near Lewes. After his announcement in 1825 of *Iguanodon*, in 1827 he announced his discovery of a second kind of dinosaur, *Hylaeosaurus*. It was heavily armoured, thus confirming that dinosaurs were pedestrians and not amphibians, as had earlier been thought.

In 1833 Mantell moved to Brighton, where he was unsuccessful in establishing a medical practice but did found the Sussex Scientific Institution and Mantellian Museum, where his home housed his collection, accompanying it with a library and reading room. When he left Brighton for London in 1838, he sold his collection for £4,000 to the British Museum, the loss to the town of 'a most intellectual ornament' opined *The Times*.

One of his last books, published in 1846, was *A Day's Ramble in and about the Antient Town of Lewes*. At his death in 1852 Mantell was credited with discovering four of the five genera of dinosaurs then known. His paleontological work was commemorated in 2000 when a monument at Whiteman's Green, Cuckfield, was unveiled. It was here in 1822 that he had discovered the *Iguanodon* fossils.

His sarcophagus in West Norwood Cemetery, London, may have been designed by his fellow Lewes townsman and Brighton resident Amon Henry Wilds.

DID YOU KNOW?

In October 1793, a clergyman in Lewes, with a single discharge of his gun, killed a partridge, shot a man and a hog, broke fourteen panes of glass in a window, knocked down six gingerbread kings and queens that were standing on a mantelpiece opposite the window, and damaged a hogstye (a pen).

Thomas Read Kemp

When his father died in 1811, Kemp succeeded him, unopposed in a by-election, as MP for Lewes, where he had been born in 1811 at No. 169 High Street (now the Barbican House Museum) on 23 December 1782, his parents' only child.

Educated at Cambridge, he married Frances Baring in 1806 and they had ten children. She died in childbirth in 1825, after which he remarried. In 1806 he purchased Herstmonceux Place, Sussex, where he and Frances lived until he sold it in 1819, and moved to Brighton.

He resigned his seat in 1816, but later became MP for Arundel, and then regained Lewes in 1826, serving in successive parliaments until 1837. He was a Whig who championed

Right: Drawing of Thomas Read Kemp by Thomas Lawrence.

Below: Thomas Kemp's birthplace, No. 169 High Street (now the Barbican House Museum). (Terry Philpot)

parliamentary reform and supported several radical measures. But he rarely took part in debates, except when they concerned Lewes or Brighton. He was a town commissioner in Brighton and welcomed William IV and Queen Adelaide when they came to Lewes on their first official visit in their coronation year of 1830.

However, like his collaborator Amon Henry Wilds, the architect, Kemp is known today for the creation of much of Regency Brighton in his role as a property speculator. Indeed, Kemp Town testifies to the fact, although his property speculation had a wider effect.

Kemp's ability to build and speculate were made possible by the lands he inherited from his father, who had himself inherited the property from an uncle in 1774. Most valuable was the freehold of nearly half the parish of Brighton outside the old town. Here, property had been spreading piecemeal since the 1770s and the town began to grow. Kemp Town was created on 40 acres of land a mile east of the old town. There was money, he believed, in creating houses of the size and elegance of those being built around Regent's Park in London to suit the very wealthy.

In his speculative ventures in Brighton, he had the architectural partnership of C. A. Busby and Amon Henry Wilds to draw up plans for the building of 106 houses. (Financial constraints cut the number from the planned 250.) In 1823, Kemp approached Thomas Cubitt to start building (he completed thirty-seven).

The building boom burst in 1824–28 and tenants were slow in completing their houses. Money ran short and it was only in the 1840s that profits started to come in, but it was too late for Kemp.

Kemp also collaborated with his brother-in-law George Baring to found an evangelical sect and set up chapels in Lewes and Brighton where Kemp preached. He returned to the Church of England in 1823, and he also returned to fashionable society, extravagant living, and politics.

He took his house in Sussex Square, Brighton, in 1827, where lived for ten years and entertained in a manner befitting his station, if not his financial situation. But he donated the site for Sussex (now the Royal) County Hospital, Brighton, and £1,000 toward its cost. This, his lifestyle and the slow growth of his enterprise had a detrimental effect on him. His mortgages amounted to at least £84,000 and his creditors were in pursuit. In April 1837 Kemp resigned as an MP, let his Kemp Town properties (the Brighton land would be auctioned in 1842), and his London house, and went to live on the continent for the rest of his life. He came back once in 1840–41. It was only eleven years after his death, in 1844, that his construction plans, as envisaged, were completed.

Amon Henry Wilds

Born in Lewes, Wilds is best known now for the extraordinary architectural legacy of Regency Brighton, much of which he created in partnership with C. A. Busby and his father, another Amon, a carpenter and builder, who was also born in the town. Wilds was baptised in 1790 at All Saints', Lewes.

The Wilds established their firm in 1806 in Lewes, and in 1815 moved to Brighton, permanently from 1820, where there was much development. He was still living in Lewes in 1818 when he submitted a design for a new road to connect Middle Street and West Street in Brighton, but the project grew and by 1821 he was supervising the construction of a raised promenade and sea wall to stretch from West Street to East Street, which would offer a direct link across the town from east to west via the seafront.

His partnership with C. A. Busby was dissolved, amid great acrimony, after only twenty-five months, but their work was extensive. (He had continued to work with his father during this time.) However, as their drawings are usually signed 'Wilds & Busby', it is difficult to distinguish who designed which building. Wilds' work, though, tends to be marked by Egyptian details, ammonite Ionic capitals, and bold scallop shells recessed over windows, and later, Italianate designs.

DID YOU KNOW?

Amon Henry Wilds would often decorate his buildings with ammonites, fossilised sea creatures that became extinct at the same time as dinosaurs. It was a pun on the fact that he and his father, a carpenter and builder with whom he collaborated, shared the same Christian name. Two ammonites appear on No. 116 High Street, Lewes, once home of Dr Richard Russell, physician and pioneer of what is now called thalassatherapy.

Ammonite capital by Amon Wilds at No. 116 High Street. (Terry Philpot)

Wilds' recreation was archery and later in his life he experimented in other areas: he invented a new way of cleaning chimneys and proposed a breakwater to protect Brighton's coastline. In 1831 he became high commissioner of Hove and helped prepare the local petition in favour of the Reform Bill. He also served as a Brighton commissioner from 1845 to 1848 (as his father had been earlier). The commissioners asked him to plant elm trees along the road to Brighton Racecourse, which became Elm Grove. He died in Shoreham in 1857.

Wynne Edwin Baxter

Baxter was born in Lewes in 1844 and trained in the law, but as a coroner he oversaw some of the most infamous cases of his day, including the victims of Jack the Ripper. In 1907 he said that he had conducted 30,000 inquests but had never required an exhumation.

His grandfather, a printer and book publisher, had moved to Lewes in 1800 and Wynne's father, William, followed in the family business in the town. (His son retained a family interest by at one time being vice-president of the Provincial Newspaper Society.) Baxter attended Lewes Old Grammar School and was also privately tutored in Brighton. He became a solicitor in 1867. Although Baxter left Lewes for London in 1875, all of his six children were born in the town and he never lost his attachment to it.

Plot of the Baxter family, Lewes Cemetery, where Wynn Edwin Baxter rests. (Terry Philpot)

Baxter retained his legal practice at No. 8 Albion Street, which was eventually taken over by his son, and having been appointed junior headborough (roughly equivalent of today's mayor) for Lewes in 1868, he became junior high constable in 1878, and the last senior high constable in 1880, the only person since 1544 to hold the post two years in succession. The next year he became Lewes' first mayor.

His array of local roles included being clerk to the Lewes Provision Market, governor of the Lewes Exhibition Fund, a member of the committee of the Lewes National Schools, and a director of the Victoria Hospital, Lewes. He also held public posts in London and was a noted antiquary and plant collector.

In 1880 Baxter was a Sussex coroner and conducted the inquest on both Percy Lefroy Mapleton, the 'railway murderer', who was hanged in Lewes Prison in 1881, and his victim Isaac Gold. He also conducted the inquest on Joseph Treves, the so-called Elephant Man, in 1890. But the most notorious crimes with which he was associated with were those perpetrated in London's East End between 1888 and 1891 by Jack the Ripper. Baxter conducted the inquests on nine of the victims (although it is only known for certain that the Ripper murdered the so called 'canonical five' in 1888).

Baxter was known for his particularly blunt questioning of witnesses. His own theory – that the Ripper, someone with 'considerable anatomical skill and knowledge', wanted to obtain female organs to sell to doctors – was soon disproved.

In 1914 and 1915 Baxter conducted inquests on eleven German spies who had been captured in the UK and tried and executed in the Tower of London.

In 1917 he held inquests into the seventy-three people who had died in the explosion at the TNT factory at Silvertown in east London. He also presided over the inquest at Poplar, east London, of twenty people who had died in the first German daylight bombing raid of London when 162 people were killed.

His last public service to the town of his birth was in the year before he died when he bought The Pells from the Abergavenny estate to present it the people of Lewes as a 'public pleasure resort'.

Baxter died at his London home in 1920. His funeral took place in his adopted Stoke Newington. He is buried in the family plot in Lewes Cemetery.

DID YOU KNOW?

Lewes once had an MP who was confined to an asylum. John Cressett Pelham came from a family with estates in Sussex, where he was born, and Shrewsbury. He became MP for Lewes in 1796 but soon the eccentricity for which he was noted became an obvious mental illness and a commission of lunacy (rather like 'sectioning' today) was taken out against him. He recovered and when he succeeded to the family estates on his father's death in 1803 he moved permanently to Shropshire. He sat again in Parliament for Shrewsbury, lost his seat and as a sign of his continuing eccentricity, for no known reason, set sail for Mauritius, where he died in 1838.

On the day of his funeral in London the blinds of private homes were drawn and the libraries in the borough of Stoke Newington were shut. In Lewes, the union flag was flown at half mast.

Lewes Man and Piltdown Man

Until 1912, Piltdown was a small, pleasant, but otherwise unremarkable Sussex village, 9 1/2 miles north of Lewes. Had it not been for Charles Dawson and others it would have continued to enjoy obscurity rather than the notoriety which they bought upon it.

Charles Dawson was born in 1864 and followed his father into the legal profession, establishing a legal practice in Uckfield in 1905, the year of his marriage, where he worked until he died in 1916.

Two years previously he had bought the substantial Castle Lodge in Castle Precincts from the Marquess of Abergavenny. The marquess believed that Dawson was buying the property on behalf of the Sussex Archeological Society, which had used it as a store for some years. (Dawson had had joined the society in 1892). Dawson and the society fell out, a rift which was never completely mended.

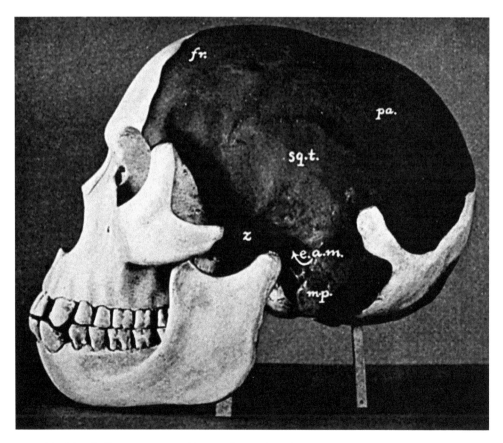

A model of the skull as reconstructed by Smith Woodward, one of the conspirators, before the hoax was exposed.

Despite professional success – he served as clerk to the Lewes magistrates for many years – Dawson's real interests were archaeology and palaeontology, which he had engaged in since childhood.

Dawson was gifted in his avocation. He was only twenty when he donated his large and valuable collection of Wealden fossils to the newly opened Natural History Museum in South Kensington. This earned him the title of honorary collector for the museum and, at twenty-one, he became a fellow of the London Geological Society. He was later responsible for the discovery of several new species of *Iguanodon*, as well as a new species of the Mesozoic mammal *Plagiaulax*.

In 1895 he was elected a fellow of the Society of Antiquaries due to his archaeological work and his two-volume *History of Hastings Castle* (1909) became a standard work.

A modest but permanent place in the annals of British science would seem to be his, rather than a legacy marked by worldwide newspaper headlines screaming scandal, and the dozens of scientific papers and books disinterring a still notorious forgery.

Between 1908 and 1912 Dawson was working in the supposedly ancient gravel bed of Barkham Manor near Piltdown. He claimed that a workman had handed him a dark-stained and thick piece of human skull that had been found in the gravels. By 1911 Dawson had collected more of the skull from around the site. With his friend Arthur Smith Woodward, the National History Museum's keeper of geology, proper excavations were made at the site in 1912 and soon more skull fragments, fossilised animal bones, primitive stone tools and a fragment of lower jaw came to light.

The remains were reconstructed toward the end of 1912 and Smith Woodward presented them to the Geological Society of London. He was convinced that this was an example of early man, the so-called 'missing link' in evolution, and named him in deference to the discoverer *Eoanthropus dawsoni* ('dawn man').

Here was, Smith Woodward and Dawson argued, Piltdown Man, the 'missing link' in human evolution, far older than any human fossil yet found in Europe. This was hailed as 'by far the most important ever made in England, and of equal, if not of greater consequence than any other discovery yet made, either at home or abroad'. But even then there was some scepticism about the match of skull and jawbone, but other finds were made, the last in 1915.

The next year, Dawson died at his home, assured of his peers' esteem for his groundbreaking work. Death at the height of his glory favoured him, as over the next forty years scepticism increased. How could one reconcile the hominid of the gravel pits with what was being revealed in the increasingly common discoveries of human fossils in Europe, Asia and Africa? Certainly, they were revealing nothing that resembled Piltdown Man. In 1953 a hoax was declared when a detailed examination, in Oxford and London, showed beyond all doubt that the Piltdown remains were faked and had been planted as part of an elaborate hoax, evidently aimed at manipulating scientific views on human evolution. Bones and artefacts from various sources had been placed on the site, most of them artificially stained to match the colour of the local gravel. The skull itself was quite recent and the jaw that of an unusually small orangutan ape with filed teeth.

Yet even as late as 1938 a memorial, paid for by public subscription, was unveiled at Barkham Manor by Sir Arthur Keith, the anatomist and anthropologist, somewhat self-interestedly as he had been one of Dawson's co-conspirators. The inscription unshamefacedly reads, 'Here in the old river gravel Mr Charles Dawson FSA found the fossil skull of Piltdown Man, 1912–13 ...'

Dawson is one of fifteen men, some eminent scientists, who have been named as culprits in a scientific conspiracy. How great his role was remains unclear but later work has associated him with other dubious finds. He was the discoverer of the first and last Piltdown remains and nothing of any significance was found after his death. His complicity seems beyond doubt and today he is known not as a paleontological pioneer but as one of the perpetrators of the greatest scientific hoax of the twentieth century.

The Piltdown conspirators, including (back row) Charles Dawson (third from the left) and Arthur Smith Woodward (fourth from left). Note the picture of Darwin behind them.

4. Up the Revolution!

It is highly unlikely that they ever met, but it is a curious quirk of history that two men, Tom Paine and James Irewell, with close associations to Lewes, should go on to play different, if significant, roles in the creation of the United States of America.

Thomas Paine

Born in Thetford, Norfolk, in 1737, and once a staymaker like his father, Thomas Paine had been an excise officer in various places before being appointed to Lewes in 1768. He would have felt at home in the town with its numerous dissenters (his father was a Quaker). He would have known of Simon de Montfort's association with the town and the fact that Anthony Stapley, MP for Lewes in 1628, had been one of those who had signed Charles I's death.

As for his work, there was much to do. The wharves at Cliffe saw groceries, wines and consumer goods arrive from London, while coal came from Newcastle and timber from the Baltic.

He lived above the fifteenth-century Bull House, the grocery and tobacco shop owned by Samuel Ollive. It would seem that Ollive, a joint constable in the town, recognised

Plaque outside the White Hart Inn, where Paine joined 'a social and intelligent circle' to debate. (Paul Lantsbury)

Above left: Thomas Paine.

Above right: Painting of Thomas Paine
in the Market Tower, Market Street.
(Paul Lantsbury)

Left: Statue of Thomas Paine outside the
library, Friary Walk. (Paul Lantsbury)

Paine's quick and independent mind. Thus, he introduced him to local society and, in particular, into membership with the Headstrong Club, a social and debating society at the White Hart Inn. Paine appears early in the town book to testify to his attending town meetings. He was also a member of St Michael's Vestry, which gave grants to the needy, levied rates and provided roads and lighting in the town.

A plaque on what is now the White Hart Hotel makes grand but not wholly exaggerated claims when it says that Paine 'here expounded his revolutionary politics', and that, 'This inn is regarded as a cradle of American independence which he helped to found with pen and sword.' Although Paine did join the Pennsylvania volunteers, he never furthered his aims by resorting to arms. As to his meetings at the inn, his biographer, Audrey Williamson, suggests the truth of this when she opines that the seeds of Paine's ideas germinated at the club.

Paine believed that the rights of Lewes' inhabitants, as elsewhere, were still 'circumscribed to the town' and the brake on the individual liberties of his compatriots was something he abhorred as much as his country's hold on its American colonies or the French monarch's repression of his subjects.

The White Hart was, said a contemporary, 'a resort of a social and intelligent circle', where Paine was 'tenacious in his opinions, which were bold, acute, and independent, and which he maintained with ardour, elegance and argument'.

On 26 March 1771, at the age of thirty-four, Paine married Elizabeth Ollive, his landlord's daughter, at St Michael's Church. Although the Ollives were members of the Westgate (then Presbyterian) Chapel, at that time nonconformist ministers could not conduct marriages. Describing himself as a 'bachelor' on the certificate, Paine may have not revealed an earlier brief marriage twelve years before, which ended with his wife's death in childbirth.

Samuel Ollive had died two years earlier, which caused Paine to leave Bull House, maybe for reasons of respectability, but he had helped Elizabeth run her father's business. Upon marriage he moved back. In accordance with his respect for individual rights, Paine gave up any claims to his wife's property, to which he was then lawfully entitled upon their marriage.

A fellow Lewes resident was Thomas 'Clio' Rickman, who was seven when Paine came to Lewes and eleven or twelve when he left. But they later became friends, so much so that Rickman published the second biography of Paine in 1819. A bookseller and publisher, Rickman's sympathies were very much the same as those of his friend – he named his sons Paine, Washington, Franklin, Rousseau, Petrarch and Volney.

Paine was a member of the Lewes Green Bowling Club and he was also so skilled a skater that he was called the Commodore. But his job was far from easy. Smuggling was common and his excise area went 10 miles to the coast at Brighthelmston (the then village of what became Brighton). He enjoyed riding over the downs and through the villages. He did not know it then but as he may have passed Firle Place, ancestral home of the Gage family. It would produce Thomas Gage, North American colonial governor and commander-in-chief of the British forces in British America, who Paine would fight to defeat. But when that time came Paine was to write his *Dialogue between General Wolfe and General Gage in a Wood near Boston*, where the latter was adjured to resign his commission if he had 'any regard for the glories of the British name'. (Gage was recalled in 1775.)

Paine is assumed to be 'Humanus', the author of a letter to the *Lewes Gazette*, who decried the fact that William Weston, declared a pauper and who was dying, had been forced to return to Keere Street as it was his native parish. At the time, the poor were forced from a parish they had settled in to their native parish to avoid the cost of keeping them falling on the adopted parish. Such action was, 'Humanus' wrote, contrary to 'the laws of God and man'.

In 1772 to 1773, Paine and other excise officers sought better pay and conditions from Parliament. This led, in 1772, to his *The Case of the Officers of Excise*, a twenty-one-page pamphlet. He distributed 4,000 copies to Parliament and the public. In London he may have met Benjamin Franklin, the US ambassador who would later give him a letter of recommendation when he travelled to the USA. Paine came back to Lewes in 1773, and the business he ran with Elizabeth collapsed. He was forced to sell household possessions to avoid debtors' prison. In 1774 he was sacked (not for the first time) by the Excise for the pamphlet.

In June of that year Paine and Elizabeth agreed to what seems to have been an amicable separation due to: 'Dissensions [that] had arisen between the said Thos. Paine and Elizabeth his wife', as a contemporary document makes clear.

His marriage failed. All but bankrupt and without a job, Paine moved to London from where, in October, he emigrated to the American colonies, arriving in Philadelphia on November 30, 1774.

Paine was quick to put his literary skills to work and in 1776 published *Common Sense*, which found the language for American resistance and was the first publication to make the case for independence in the twenty-five editions which alone appeared in 1776. Then came *The American Crisis*, with ideas developed later still in *The Rights of Man*. The USA's second president John Adams said, 'Without the pen of the author of *Common Sense*, the sword of Washington would have been raised in vain.'

Paine held a variety of official positions and then returned to England, devoting himself to science and writing the two-part *Rights of Man*. He first went to France in 1787 hoping to garner interest in building an iron bridge of his design. It was eventually erected experimentally in a field in London and then taken down. He left England for France again in 1792, partly to escape arrest for seditious libel and also because he had been elected to the French Revolutionary National Convention. (His book was banned and he was found guilty and banished *in absentia*.) His ideas, on taxation, education and social reform, including pensions as well as suffrage and animal rights, predated their realisation in the UK, in some cases more than a century after his death.

In France he saw his ideals corrupted by the Reign of Terror and he opposed the execution of the king and queen. Imprisoned for ten months, he fled back to England and was tried for the blasphemy of his *Age of Reason*. Hard up and disappointed in receiving no public post from the US government, he went to America in 1802 where he fell out with some old friends over his religious opinions. He continued to write and enjoyed the friendship of President Thomas Jefferson, whom he had known in Paris when the latter was ambassador. Paine died in New York in 1809.

There is both a plaque and lettering on Bull House. Another plaque is in Castle Precincts near the Battle of Lewes viewing place ('Resident of Lewes, Citizen of the World'). A portrait of Paine, pointing to the New World, by Julian Bell, adorns the Market Tower, Market Street. The tower was built in 1792, by which time Paine's dreams of a United States of America had been realised and in which year the French Republic was proclaimed.

James Iredell

Iredell's role in the new United States was an important one but less historically significant than that of Paine, though his writings, too, contributed to independence.

Born in Lewes in 1751, he was the oldest of the five surviving children of James Iredell, a Bristol merchant, and his Irish-born wife Margaret McColloh. His grandfather was a clergyman and Iredell was a devout Anglican (later Episcopalian), who had an interest in spirituality and metaphysics.

When his father suffered a stroke and his business failed, fifteen-year-old Iredell dropped out of school to support the family, but two years later he emigrated to the colonies. Like Paine, he too became a customs official. His mother's American relatives were well-placed and one held the sinecure of comptroller at the port of Edenton, North Carolina. He succeeded his relative in 1774 and held the post until 1776 on the outbreak of the War of Independence, working under Samuel Johnston, later governor of North Carolina. The work was not arduous and most of his pay he sent to his mother. To give himself a second career he studied law and was admitted to the bar in 1771. Two years later Iredell married Johnston's sister Hannah with whom he had three surviving children.

Iredell was an employee of the colonial government, but when he studied the constitutional aspects of the relationship between the colony and Westminster, he came to the conclusion that British actions were against the British constitution and the UK's writ unjust. His pamphlet of 1774, *To the Inhabitants of Great Britain* and *Principles of an American Whig*, set out his ideas.

Not flinching from his support for his adoptive country, the break in 1776 was a painful one: he was cut off from his mother and brothers and disinherited by a wealthy uncle in the West Indies.

James Iredell.

He became a member of the state's superior court in 1777 and two years later was appointed the state's attorney-general.

He was not above criticising the new revolutionary regime; he found fault in North Carolina not complying with all the terms of the peace and he also believed that the states should strengthen the authority of the Continental Congress under the constitution of the USA adopted in 1781. However, he was an advocate of the sovereignty of states. In 1787 he was appointed commissioner by the state assembly, with the task of compiling and revising the state laws. This saw the light of day in 1791 as *Iredell's Revisal*.

George Washington was impressed by Iredell's reputation as a jurist and legal scholar and also wanted a Southern Supreme Court justice to strengthen the union, and so nominated Iredell as associate justice of the Court in February 1790, the appointment being confirmed in May. At thirty-eight, he is youngest Supreme Court justice ever to have been appointed.

In the early days of the court the work was not burdensome and, indeed, it did not hear its first case until 1791. In Iredell's day, as well as its two annual terms in Washington DC, it was also required that the justices travel twice a year to hear cases and appeals in various circuit courts or courts of appeal in each of the then thirteen states.

The burden of travel affected Iredell's health and he died suddenly, at the age of forty-eight, on 20 October 1799. A slave owner who was opposed to the institution, he was a kindly master who freed many of his slaves.

DID YOU KNOW?

Lewes' association with the United States is not limited to Tom Paine and James Iredell. William Penn, who was to become the founder of Pennsylvania, married as his first wife Gulielma Maria Springett, the daughter of Sir William Springett, of Broyle Place, Ringmer, Sussex, a parliamentary officer who died at the siege of Arundel Castle. The lands of Delaware were given to Penn by Charles II as payment of a debt owed to Penn's father. He renamed the town of Hoernkills, Lewes, and made it the county seat of Sussex County.

John Stansfield, a shipping merchant of Cliffe and grandfather of the diarist John Evelyn of Southover Grange, built the Church of St Michael the Archangel, South Malling, and eight-year-old John laid one of the first stones in 1626. It was at this church on 19 April 1636 that the London-born Revd John Harvard married Anne Sadler, daughter of the vicar of neighbouring Ringmer. The couple lived in London, and in 1637 they embarked for New England. Harvard died there a year later, making a deathbed bequest to the 'schoale or Colledge' at Cambridge, recently undertaken by the Massachusetts Bay Colony, of his library of more than 400 volumes and £800. It was in gratitude that the institution is now known as Harvard University. It was the first college to experiment with the co-education of Native Americans alongside white people.

Had Tom Paine and his contemporaries' efforts not proved fruitful, then there would be no need to mention that in 1643 Judith Fuller of Southover and Henry Soane of Lilington, 9 miles from Lewes, were licensed to be married at St John-sub-Castro (Saxon predecessor of the present church on the site) in Abinger Place. But as the revolutionaries did prevail, it can be remarked that Judith and Henry were great-great-grandparents of Thomas Jefferson, third president of the USA.

Above: Statue of John Harvard,
Harvard University, Massachusetts.

Right: William Penn.

Eamon de Valera

Revolutionaries with far less freedom of movement in Lewes than Paine or Iredell were the Irish rebels of the Easter Rising confined in Lewes Prison in 1916. Their leader was Eamon de Valera, later the new country's prime minister and its longest-serving president, who had been spared execution but was sentenced to penal servitude for life. The others included Harry Boland, who was to die in the Irish Civil War, Joseph McGuinness, who was to be elected an MP while serving his sentence, Frank Lawless, who would be elected to the Irish parliament, and Thomas Ashe.

De Valera's activities separated him from his impoverished wife and small children. He and his colleagues had been in Dartmoor and were transferred to Lewes from a short stay in Maidstone on 13 November for their part in the ill-fated Easter Rising of 1916. (It was in Lewes that de Valera read his full account of the rising in an Italian pamphlet.) The prison had better conditions than the other two prisons: wooden floors replaced flagstones and prisoners could talk freely when exercising.

The men's transfer was an attempt by the new prime minister, Lloyd George, to placate Irish-American opinion (the USA not having entered the First World War at this time). The disadvantage for the British was that all the Irishmen were under one roof.

A mathematics teacher by profession, de Valera had risen in the ranks of the Irish volunteers, but prison seems to have brought out his talents for leadership, as he became defiant in standing up to the prison authorities, although he had been recognised as the men's leader in Dartmoor. When first held in Lewes, they were in solitary confinement, but after they elected de Valera their commandant, they were able to mix. Among the improved reading material available in Lewes was the *Catholic Bulletin* through which de Valera could calculate that the amount of calories in the prisoners' food allowance was inadequate and

Eamon de Valera.

DID YOU KNOW?

In March 2016, the prison diary of Eamon de Valera, later Irish prime minister and president, written in Dartmoor, Maidstone, and Lewes prisons in 1916, was auctioned in Dublin for 5,400 euros. It was a gift from prisoner Q95 – de Valera – to Michael Veale, a War of Independence veteran. The anonymous vendor had purchased it from Kathleen, Veale's widow, in 1971.

so organised a petition for the food to be improved. As a result, the prisoners were served kippered herring three times a week. When a prisoner was put on bread and water for talking while working, de Valera ordered all the men to stop work. The man was released.

In May 1917 he led the men in a protest to receive prisoner of war status and to do no labour other than that which served them. They were confined to their cells. When they set to work to destroy prison windows and lamps, the prison authorities decided to separate them. Some went to Pentonville in London and de Valera and others seen as ring leaders were returned to Maidstone. But the stay was short, as they were to be released as part of a general amnesty.

In Lewes, de Valera was anxious to play as much as a part as he could in the events in Ireland, not least the contentious issue of whether elections should be contested. It was when they were being sent back to Dublin in June 1917 that de Valera received the news that he had been selected to stand in the East Clare by-election, which he won the next month. He was to be jailed again by the British in Lincoln Prison – by then he was president of Sinn Fein – but he escaped to take part in the War of Independence.

John Maynard Keynes

A man whose ideas had a profound effect on the world but of a different kind to Paine, Iredell and the Irish rebels was the economist, writer, government adviser and art collector John Maynard Keynes. He was to reshape the economies of much of the Western world with his ideas, known as Keynesianism, expressed in his *The General Theory on Employment, Interest and Money* (1936).

He and his wife, the ballerina Lydia Lopokova, had a house in Gordon Square, Bloomsbury, along with other members of the Bloomsbury Group, like Leonard and Virginia Woolf.

Keynes had grown to know Sussex, especially during the First World War when he had spent most weekends, for six months, in south-east of Lewes at Charleston, the home of his friends, the painter Vanessa Bell, her art critic husband Clive Bell and her lover, the painter Duncan Grant. He would come down from London on a Friday or a Saturday evening.

In March 1926, Keynes and Lopokova took possession of nearby Tilton House on a twenty-one-year lease at £130 a year. He was to enjoy at Tilton 'the happiest and most productive months' for the remainder of his life, as Robert Skidelsky, his biographer says.

John Maynard Keynes (left)
and his friend Kingsley Martin,
editor of the *New Statesman*.

The house was a two-storey farmhouse set in several acres of lawn, orchard and woodland, and though plain, it was surprisingly spacious. Unusually for the time, it was served by electricity and had a telephone. Early on, Keynes created a library and a loggia. There were six staff and in a cottage in the grounds lived the chauffeur/gardener and his wife, the housekeeper. With a new lease in 1935, he commissioned a rebuilding 'on a magnificent scale', he said, with a new wing, a bathroom for each guest, servants' quarters and a large, new staircase.

It was only a walk across the downs from Charleston, and Vanessa's sister, Virginia Woolf, and her husband Leonard Woolf, lived a short car journey away in Rodmell. But while Keynes adored Lydia, a renowned ballerina who was proud of the peasant stock from which she came, the Bloomsburyites tended to look down on her. But Tilton was a happy home where Keynes and Lydia played tennis and entertained friends.

Tilton was a place of rest and relaxation, where the London friendships could be continued, but it was also a principal place of residence when Keynes was not at Cambridge University or London. At Tilton he wrote his *Treatise on Money* and worked on his *General Theory*. He said, 'There is no better place to work.'

Keynes took a lively interest in Lewes. When the Revd Kenneth Rawlings became vicar of St Michael's Church in 1925, and found that Lewes had had no theatre for 100 years, he formed The Players, who performed in St Michaels' Hall and the Town Hall successfully until 1939. When he tried to create a theatre, some inhabitants were opposed and some of his congregation left because of his pacifism. But Keynes not only supported him but lent £125 toward the purchase price of the Old Chapel in Lancaster Street, which was being used as a vehicle repair shop at that time. Keynes' work for the theatre was especially generous because at that time his investments had tumbled due to the threat of war and his income fell by a third to £6,192 in 1938–39. He also became a trustee of the appeal to raise £5,000 for the project. Although only £76 came in, Keynes, Rawlings and others brought the Lewes Little Theatre into being in 1939. This and the coincidental opening of the Miller Centre, a gallery and arts centre, caused Duncan Grant to refer to Lewes as 'the Athens of the South'.

Another local practical example of Keynes' generosity was his helping to fund the murals in nearby Berwick Church, painted by Bell and Grant in 1942–43.

Tilton House proved a godsend when, in 1937, Keynes was taken seriously ill with subacute bacterial endocarditis, spending six months in Ruthin Castle in north Wales, then a sanatorium. When he left there in February 1938, he returned to recuperate in Tilton House, often sleeping all day according to Lydia. Conditions were comparatively primitive: when their private well ceased to serve them Lydia remarked, in 1938, that she and no one else had had a bath for a month. They had farm labourers dig a new well.

Keynes was never a countryman. Skidelsky says that he played at being a member of the squirearchy. But he used to like to walk across the Downs and also shoot – in 1941 one party bagged twenty-eight peasants, four rabbits, one hare, two woodcocks, and a sparrowhawk.

Keynes came back exhausted from the USA in 1946 having negotiated preferential treatment for US loans for the rebuilding of the British economy. During this last illness he went on his final journey by car up Firle Beacon and walked down, something he had not done for years. The next day, Easter Sunday, 21 April 1946, he died of a heart attack in bed at Tilton House; his ashes were scattered on the Downs above his home.

However, his brother Geoffrey had overlooked Keynes' stipulation in his will that his ashes should be placed in the chapel of King's College, Cambridge, but they now lie where he had found both peace and creativity.

DID YOU KNOW?

St Michael's Church, High Street, was founded in Norman times and its round tower is one of 185 in the country and only one of three in Sussex, the others being in Piddinghoe and Southease.

5. Fine Arts: Art, Music and Literature

The madrigalists, Southover Grange Gardens. (Terry Philpot)

Lewes' main claim to fame in arts and literature derives from some of the very contrasting people who have had associations with the town – among them writers as different as Virginia Woolf and Daisy Ashcroft. But its earliest artistic luminary was a musician born in the sixteenth century – the magrigalist Nicholas Yonge.

Nicholas Yonge

We do not know when or where Yonge was born in the town, only that he died in 1619. His mother's name was Bray. He must still have been a young man when he moved to London to live in the parish of St Michael, Cornhill. He resided there for some years because seven of his nine children were baptised there and, indeed, he was buried there. He became vicar-choral of St Paul's Cathedral in 1592.

Yonge's lasting legacy is as the editor of two anthologies of mostly Italian vocal music. These were published, with English texts, as *Musica transalpina* in 1588 and 1597.

The first volume was international in scope and contains fifty-seven madrigals. This was the first recorded use in English of the term and applies not only to actual madrigals, but also to chansons, canzonets and other musical forms. He also sought pieces written in the vernacular, when much was in Italian, which many people did not speak.

The importance of Yonge's anthologies lies in his having popularised the form in England. This allowed Elizabethan composers to imitate the continental models and create an indigenous madrigal. He made his will on 19 October 1619, four days before he was buried.

There is a charming statue of madrigal singers, dedicated to Yonge, by Austin Bennett, in Southover Grange Gardens.

John Evelyn

Evelyn set in train Lewes' remarkable literary tradition as the greatest English diarist after his contemporary Samuel Pepys. He was born in 1620 in Wotton, Surrey, on the 700-acre family estate. His father Richard became High Sheriff of Sussex and Surrey in 1633. Evelyn went to stay with his maternal grandparents in Cliffe when he was five. In Lewes, Evelyn began to draw and sketch before he even went to school in 1630. He began to keep notes the following year, which became the genesis of his diary.

His father's wish to send him to Eton was overcome by his son pleading to be allowed to continue his education at the grammar school, then in Garden Street, a plea occasioned

Southover Grange, childhood home of John Evelyn.

partly because he liked living with his 'too indulgent' grandmother, who had remarried, and so he moved with her to Southover Grange (said to have been built for William Newton from the Caen stone of the Lewes Priory in 1572). In Evelyn's time the gardens (now a very pleasant public park) would have been far more extensive, with a paddock and an avenue of trees and a circular carriage turning outside the entrance.

In 1637 he and two of his brothers were admitted to the Middle Temple. The same year, Evelyn was admitted fellow-commoner of Balliol College, Oxford, but he left without a degree, which was not unusual then for young men of his class.

The diary (more properly notes) he may have begun in the same sort of almanac that he used for the year 1637 but the form in which his work is now available was not created until the 1860s. Many of the entries about the Continent (where he travelled extensively, in part as a soldier, from 1641) make use of later guidebooks that refer to things Evelyn could not have seen himself. There is much personal reflection and also what is more like today's news reporting.

Evelyn's reputation as a scholar came later. He is now seen as someone whose voluminous correspondence did much to exchange scientific ideas. His interest in horticulture, expressed in his garden at the 200-acre Sayers Court, Deptford, with his attendant writings on the subject, contributed much to English landscape gardening in the eighteenth century.

James Lambert

James Lambert was probably five (he was baptised at the end of 1725) when he moved with his parents, John and Susan, and his seven brothers and sisters, from Willingdon in Sussex to Cliffe, and he grew up at No. 1 South Street (now the Bag of Books children's bookshop).

Lambert was educated in the town, took instruction from a music master and from 1745 until he died he was the parish organist at the Church of St Thomas à Becket. He also published volumes of psalms and at one time taught music. He worked as a sign painter and a gilder and in 1758 was a stationer.

Were this not enough, his ambition was to be a landscape painter and it is possible that after he married in 1760 he took instruction. Between 1768 and 1773 he was exhibiting at the Free Society of Artists and then at the Royal Academy between 1774 and 1778. His canvases were often of rural scenes. In 1770 the Society of Arts awarded him 15 guineas for one of them.

The family of his nephew, James, owned No. 2 Chapel Hill, around the corner, from 1782 to 1795, but there is no evidence that any of them lived there. James Jr, described as a 'coach and sign painter, herald and landscape painter', was less talented than his uncle, but assisted him in cashing in on the fashion for topographical watercolours. Local landowners employed Lambert to paint pictures of their homes. One patron, Dr William Burrell, bequeathed 269 watercolours by the Lamberts to the British Museum.

All in all more than 700 pictures have been attributed to them, but some are not easy to distinguish as they both signed themselves 'James Lambert', while some the uncle did not sign but allowed his nephew to sign. Their work ranges from pencil sketches to watercolours and oils of Sussex churches, abbeys, castles and country houses. They can

Home of James Lambert, now the Bag of Books children's bookshop, No. 1 South Street. (Paul Lantsbury)

'Figures with a donkey and a dog crossing a weir' by James Lambert.

be seen in places as diverse as Brighton Museum and Art Gallery to the Yale Centre for British Art, and the Victoria and Albert Museum to the Sussex Archeological Society. The elder James never realised his ambition to paint imaginary landscapes in oils for his diffident character was ill-suited to the art world of London, which would have been key to such achievement.

Lambert died in 1788 in penurious circumstances, such that administration of his estate was granted to his creditors. He was survived by his wife, as their one child had died in infancy. He was buried at St John-sub-Castro Church, as the church at Cliffe had no graveyard. His nephew was also to be buried there (he died in 1799) and there are memorials to the two of them on the outer wall of the chancel.

But whatever his last financial circumstances or his limitations, Lambert earned his place in the history of art in the county as the first painter in east Sussex to be an artist rather than just an artisan.

Alice Dudeney

Alice Dudeney suffers a fate not uncommon by some who attain great acclaim in their lifetimes – she is virtually unknown today. A novelist and short story writer under the name Mrs Henry Dudeney, she wrote more than fifty books.

Born in 1866, her portrayals of Sussex life, especially of the working and lower middle classes, caused her to be compared to Thomas Hardy. Her best known works are *A Man with a Maid* (1897), *Folly Corner* (1899), *Maternity of Harriott Wicken* (1899) and *Spindle and Plough* (1901). Her books are strongly realistic, often tackling matters such as marriage difficulties (including bigamy), sexual abuse, and unmarried pregnancy – subjects difficult to write about in her day, especially so by a woman.

London-born, Brighton-raised and Hurstpierpoint-educated, in 1883 she married Henry Dudeney, an inventor of problems and mathematical puzzles, in London. The death of their first child at four months caused her to stop writing for a while. She then worked for a publisher and her short stories began to appear.

When their daughter Mary was born in 1890, the Dudeneys moved from London to near Billingshurst and then bought land in Surrey, creating a country estate called Littlewick Meadow, which needed several servants to run it.

However, despite increasing success and wealth and moving in high social circles (she was friendly with Sir Philip Sassoon and his sister, Sybil), she had marital troubles of her own, exacerbated by her affair with the artist Paul Hardy. Her *A Lewes Diary 1919-1944* (1998) describes the vicissitudes of the marriage. She and Henry separated and Littlewick Meadow was sold. But when Mary emigrated to Canada, the couple were reconciled and moved to Lewes, buying Brack Mound House (then Castle Precincts House), Castle Precincts, in 1921. (The house is now divided into two properties, one of which bears the name.) They later lived in the Old Poor House, No. 7 Castle Banks. At one time she also owned No. 138 High Street, Nos 1–6 Mount Cottages and cottages in Westgate Street, which were rented.

Henry died in 1930 and Alice remained in the town. She continued to write until 1937. She suffered a stroke and died on 21 November 1945. An eighteenth-century Sussex sandstone obelisk, which she had copied, marks their shared grave in Lewes Cemetery.

MRS. HENRY DUDENEY

Alice Dudeney.

The Old Poor House, Castle Banks, home of
Alice Dudeney. (Paul Lantsbury)

Brack Mount House, Castle Precincts, home of Alice Dudeney. (Terry Philpot)

Virginia Woolf

Monk's House, Rodmell, which Virginia Woolf shared with her writer husband Leonard, is only 4 1/2 miles from Lewes and has become a shrine for enthusiasts for her work. However, Woolf has a curious and less well-known connection with Lewes through the Round House – the home she owned but never lived in. The charmingly eccentric house is bounded by the western wall of the castle in Pipe Passage.

In 1919 the lease on Asheham House, the Woolfs' home 4 miles south of Lewes, near Little Talland, had come to an end and they were looking for somewhere nearby that was close to Charleston, the house where Woolf's sister, Vanessa Stephen, lived. (Asheham House, uninhabited for many years, was demolished in 1994.)

The Round House was part of a windmill until 1819 when the then owner, William Smart, removed the smock (the weatherboarded tower), the sweeps (the sails) and the workings to a new site near the barracks, where Lewes Prison now stands. It was known as the Mill House in 1891 and it is not known if what later became the Round House was immediately converted into a house, but an early print of unknown date shows that a thatched roof was added.

After visiting a local estate agent, Virginia greeted her discovery of the house with enthusiasm. In her diary on 9 June 1919 she wrote,

> Off I went up Pipes [sic: it lost the 's' in 1938] Passage, under the clock, & saw rising at
> the top of the sloping path a singular shaped roof, rising to a point, & spreading out in

Virginia Woolf.

The Round House, Pipe Passage, the home of Virginia Woolf, which she never lived in. (Paul Lantsbury)

a circular petticoat all round it ... An elderly and humble cottage woman, the owner, showed me over. How far my satisfaction with small rooms, & the view, & the ancient walls, & the wide sitting room, & the general oddity & character of the whole place were the result of finding something that would do, that one could conceive living in, & that was cheap (freehold £300) I don't know; but as I inspected the rooms I became conscious of a rising desire to settle here; to have done with looking about; to take this place, & make it one's permanent lodging... I liked the way the town dropped from the garden leaving us on a triangular island, vegetables on one side, grass on the other; the path encircling the round house [*sic*] amused me; nor are we overlooked. In short, I took it there & then... Lewes that afternoon, with its many trees & laburnums, & water meadows, & sunny bow windows, & broad High Street looked very tempting & dignified. ... we ... are now secure of a lodging on earth so long as we need sleep or sit anywhere.

'Very old, small but rather charming', is how she described it in a letter to Vanessa and it was so tempting that she bought it for £300 without even consulting Leonard. When Leonard was able to visit a few weeks later, he was unenthusiastic (they were after all seeking a home in the country) and they decided it was not for them.

When the Woolfs were in Lewes, they saw an advertisement for Monk's House. It suited them better in every way, but Virginia expressed herself, in her diary, as 'loyal to the Round House'. She cycled to Rodmell the day after that Lewes visit and purchased the new house for £700. They made a profit on the Lewes house. It went to a John Every for £320 'so we shan't lose anything over it; I believe if we had risked waiting we could have got £400', she confided to Vanessa.

Daisy Ashford

A writer whose attachment to Lewes was far less fleeting than that of Woolf, and, indeed, who wrote her most famous book there, was Daisy Ashford. She wrote *The Young Visiters* (*sic*: although Ashford's original spelling was 'Viseters') when she was eight or nine and living in Southdown House, No. 44 St Anne's Crescent. Her family had moved there in 1889, from Petersham, Hampshire, where Daisy had been born, when she was eight.

The Ashfords were Catholics who attended mass at the Church of St Pancras, Irelands Lane. Neighbours included the Robsons, one of whom, Harriet, had married the Catholic convert poet and critic Coventry Patmore and became his third wife. He would visit the Ashfords when old and in ill health and sit on their sofa while Daisy's mother Emma read aloud to him.

Daisy was educated mostly at home with two of her sisters. She wrote a story, *The Life of Father McSwiney*, dictated to her father, when she was four (it appeared in 1983). Later she wrote other stories, a play and one short novel, *The Hangman's Daughter*, which she thought her best. At four Daisy wrote with a mature hand that could have been that of an adult. The window to the left at the rear of the house is the nursery where she wrote. She and her sisters had been encouraged to write as children (Emma was accomplished at writing verse).

In 1896 the family moved to the Wallands area of the town and then to Bexhill.

The Young Visiters remains in print and was written in an exercise book which lay in a draw for twenty-seven years before seeing the light of day. Ashford was thirty-six when,

Right: Daisy Ashford.

Below: Southdown House, St Anne's Crescent, where Daisy Ashford wrote *The Little Visiters*. (Terry Philpot)

in 1917, she came upon her manuscript while she and her sisters were sorting out their mother's papers after she had died. It was full of spelling mistakes and each chapter was written as a single paragraph.

Ashford lent the exercise book to Margaret Mackenzie, who showed it to the novelist Frank Swinnerton, a reader for Chatto & Windus. He was so taken with this piece of juvenilia that he wanted to publish it. (Ashford was working for the British Legation in Berne when she learned.) Swinnerton secured a preface from J. M. Barrie. Barrie wrote of a photograph of the author as a child, which appeared in the book:

> This is no portrait of a writer who had to burn the oil at midnight (indeed, there is documentary evidence that she was hauled off to bed every evening at six): it has the air of careless power; there is a complacency about it that by the severe might perhaps be called smugness. It needed no effort for that face to knock off a masterpiece.

Reviewers like A. A. Milne and Robert Graves enthused about the book and the public reaction was such that it was reprinted eighteen times in its first year but not without rumours, which persisted for years, that this was a literary hoax perpetrated by Barrie himself.

Remarkably, given not only her age but her middle-class origins, the book was set in high Victorian society. With perhaps understandable exaggeration, the poet Edward Lucie-Smith wrote of her: 'In her own way, Daisy was a phrase maker on par with Oscar Wilde.'

A year after publication, the book became a stage play that was adapted for New York audience. In 1968 it was turned into a musical, in 1984 into a film and in 2003 into a BBC television film. There were illustrated editions in 1949 and 1984.

Shy and self-effacing, Ashford could never understand the fame that came her way. In a preface to *Daisy Ashford: Her Book* (1920) she wrote, 'I can never feel all the nice things that have been said about *The Young Visiters* are really due to me at all, but to a Daisy Ashford of so long ago that she seems almost another person.'

Ashford gave up writing in her teens (although her daughter said that she continued to tell exciting stories) and moved to London, where she worked as a secretary, and then ran a canteen in Dover during the First World War. In 1920, when several of her short stories were published, she married and settled in Norfolk, where she and her husband ran a cut-flowers business and later a pub. She began an autobiography in her old age, which she later destroyed. She died in 1972.

Eve Garnett

Like Daisy Ashford, Eve Garnett was also a children's writer who remains best known for one book, *The Family at One End Street*, although she wrote several others. Garnett moved to Lewes when she was thirty-four.

Born to a wealthy family in Worcestershire in 1900, she was partly educated at home and then at a convent school in Devon. She moved with her family to various addresses before moving back to Worcestershire. At one time she lived with her married sister in India (in what is now Pakistan). Unmarried, she came to Lewes in 1934 and lived at various addresses in or near the town for the rest of her life before settling at No. 12 Keere Street, Lewes, from 1960 to 1988.

Home of Eve Garnett in Keere
Street. (Terry Philpot)

When Garnett came back from India in 1921, she trained as an artist and was successful enough to exhibit in London. But from childhood she had a growing consciousness of poverty through reading and observation. Her early writing and painting is an empathetic reflection of these concerns.

The Family from One End Street was published in 1937, and the following year won the prestigious Carnegie Medal for the writer of an outstanding children's book. It is the story of Mr and Mrs Ruggles, a working-class couple who work hard and struggle to provide for their eight children. It relates positively the small family events of working-class life with a strong awareness of community and striving to make life better.

The novel broke away from both stereotyping the working class and the conventions of children's fiction, which tended to feature nannies, nurseries, country houses and boarding schools.

Further Adventures of the Family from One End Street came out in 1956 and Garnett published *Holiday at the Dew Drop Inn* in 1962. However, by that time there had been a change in the critical view of the book, now seen as over-sentimental in how it represented working-class life. In 1968 she published *To Greenland's Icy Mountains*, a biography of the Norwegian explorer and missionary Hans Egede. This stemmed from her long connection with Norway, which she visited twelve times from 1936 onwards. Garnett continued to write up to the publication of *First Affections: Some Autobiographical Chapters of Early Childhood*, published in 1982.

In 1988 Garnett moved to the Greenacre Residential Home, Lewes Road, Ringmer. She died at the Victoria Hospital, Nevill Road, Lewes, on 5 April 1991.

Val Gielgud and Sir John Drummond

A consideration of Lewes' arts community would not be complete without reference to two luminaries of the BBC, both of whom spent many years in its service, with each branching out to other endeavours.

Sir John Drummond came to Lewes in 1997 after his retirement to live with his partner Bob Lockyer, who had bought a cottage in the town. He later lived at No. 3 Caburn Court, Station Street, a retirement complex. Very little is known of his time in the town (he makes no mention of it in his autobiography *Tainted by Experience,* published three years after his move).

While he was one of the great cultural impresarios of the twentieth century, he enjoyed a sometimes fractious relationship with the BBC, as he did with some colleagues. His sarcasm was legendary and David Attenborough described his 'unlimited capacity for indignation'. John Kenyon, who succeeded him at Radio 3, wrote of 'the warm, responsive humanity beneath the bluster'.

In 1964 Drummond was part of the launch team for BBC2 and became head of arts for the channel. He also served as a television producer, broadcaster and controller (music), and controller of Radio 3. For five years he was also a very successful director of the Edinburgh Festival and was director of the Proms for ten seasons.

When he left Radio 3 in 1992 he became particularly critical of the regime of the then director-general John Birt, who, he said, had created an organisation that followed society, rather than led taste, adding, 'I see no reason for its existence.'

His last years were made very difficult by a mysterious illness that affected his spine, making walking difficult and preventing him attending concerts, which had been such a joy in his life. A respite of a couple of years allowed him to again indulge in travel and for his seventieth birthday he celebrated in Lewes with friends in some style. When he died of multi-organ failure at the Royal Sussex County Hospital, Brighton, on 6 September 2006, Lockyer was at his bedside.

Val Gielgud, brother of Sir John Gielgud, lived at Wychwood, Church Road, Barcombe, near Lewes, from at least the mid-sixties until his death at the age of eighty-one in 1981. His BBC career was a wide one. He was appointed director of drama in 1929 and retired as head of sound drama after thirty-five years. In between times, he was seconded to work in fledgling television. He also directed the first television drama, Pirandello's *The Man with the Flower in his Mouth.*

During his time with the BBC he also wrote novels, including detective fiction, stage plays, broadcast plays (in which he very occasionally acted) and collaborated on several film scenarios, including *Death at Broadcasting House*, in which he acted. He was married five time and in *Who's Who* listed one hobby as 'enjoying the company of Siamese cats'.

DID YOU KNOW?

Albion Russell was a boot and shoe manufacturer, with a double-fronted shop in 1861 at the junction of Fisher Street (where he has a commemorative plaque) and High Street in what is now the visitors' centre. In 1873 he took on George Frederick Bromley, as a journeyman-shoemaker. In 1874 Bromley married the boss's daughter, Elizabeth. When, six years later, the couple took over management of Russell's shop in Eastbourne, Russell & Bromley appeared over the door for the first time. When Albion died in 1888, Elizabeth inherited the Eastbourne shop, but her brother Albion took over those in Lewes, Newhaven and East Grinstead. The Bromley family still retain control of the company.

6. Art for Art's Sake: The Story of Two Artistic Communities

Few of Lewes' writers and artists led wholly conventional lives, but the most unconventional, in very different ways, were Eric Gill, sculptor, typographer and wood carver, and the American art connoisseur Edward Perry Warren. Both set up residential communities – Gill in Ditchling and Perry in Lewes – for the promotion of art.

Eric Gill

Gill was born in Brighton in 1882, enjoying a childhood that his biographer Fiona McCarthy describes as an unusually happy one but 'moralistic, strict, emotional, cosy and contained' and one of 'amiable primness'. His father was a clergyman. This is the very opposite of what we now know of much of Gill's adult life, which was revealed forty-nine years after his death.

Educated in the nursery at home when he was six, Gill was sent to a kindergarten. He was a slow learner and, ironically, given his later career as a typographer, at eight he could only read three-letter words. He then attended a local boys' day school. Gill's

The Ditchling Museum of Art and Craft, which displays much work by Eric Gill and his associates. (Ditchling Museum of Art and Craft)

childhood was a 'fairly happy' but he was an indifferent scholar, apart from arithmetic, and unexceptional for one who was so rebellious as an adult. He was also keen on cricket.

Although the family moved to Chichester when Eric was fourteen, it was in Brighton in 1913 that the most significant event of his life occurred – his reception, with his wife Ethel (Ettie), into the Catholic Church.

This led to the creation, in 1921, in Ditchling, 7 miles north of Lewes, of the Guild of St Joseph and St Dominic, with Hilary Pepler, writer, poet and printer, and Desmond Chute, engraver and later a priest. One of its early members was David Jones, the poet and painter. The guild, while specifically Catholic, was based on the idea of the medieval guild, which existed for the protection and the promotion of its members' work and had been revived by the leaders of the Arts and Crafts movement. It was a lay religious order with an artistic calling, a self-sufficient community of work, faith and domestic life, with workshops and a chapel. It was, in part, a reaction against modern life and industrialisation after the First World War. It was also all-male – no women were admitted until 1971.

Gill moved in 1907 to 'Soper's' and in 1913 moved to Hopkin's Crank on Ditchling Common, 2 miles north of the village.

And while Gill began wearing a girdle of chastity under a habit, his personal diaries describe his sexual activity in great detail, including extramarital affairs, incest with his two eldest teenage daughters, and incestuous relationships with his sisters. In 1924 Gill left to found a new community at Capel-y-ffin in Wales. Despite his behaviour and his eccentricities, the guild left behind a remarkable body of work – some of it public, as can be seen, for example, in Gill's Stations of the Cross in Westminster Cathedral, and at the Ditchling Museum of Art and Craft, Lodge Hill Lane.

Gill died in 1940 and is buried at Princes Risborough, Buckinghamshire, where his community found its last home, surviving until 1989.

Edward Perry Warren

Like Gill, Warren, a wealthy American expatriate, founded an artistic community, known as the Lewes House Brotherhood, but, in purpose and tone, it differed vastly from that set up by the promiscuous sculptor, Eric Gill. There were very strong elements of homoeroticism in the brotherhood and Warren sought to normalise gay relationships in the way matters were in ancient Greece. Some artworks he collected were very explicitly homoerotic. To advocate his ideas his books, all pseudonymously published, included *A Tale of Pausanian Love* in 1927 and the privately printed three volumes of *A Defence of Uranian Love*, between 1928 and 1930.

Known as Ned and born in 1860, the third son of Samuel Denis Warren of Massachusetts, founder of the Cumberland Paper Mills in Maine, Warren was educated at Harvard. He later entered Oxford, which was more tolerant of his homosexuality, and read Classics.

His earliest interest was antiquities – particularly Grecian. He followed his parents in becoming a great collector of pictures, fine arts and china. After his father's death and having little interest in the family business, Warren settled permanently in England and sought a large property. Staying at the White Hart on 22 October 1889, he wrote of Lewes House in the High Street to his friend John Marshall, who was to join him in the venture:

> The house that may do here is huge, old and not cheap. It has only three or four sunny rooms (this number might be just sufficient), and then a goodly number of large north rooms. It is in the centre of Lewes and yet has a quiet garden, a big kitchen garden, paddock, a greenhouse and stables ad lib. You can also have a walk by the seaside. I am much inclined to it.

In 1890 he moved into his new home, which dates from 1733, with Marshall (who married in 1907, much to Warren's distress). At first living there on a long lease of £150 a year, Warren bought the property in 1913 for £3,750.

Over thirty-eight years Warren enabled Lewes to become an international centre for art collecting, as he travelled widely in pursuit of works of art. Many of his acquisitions have enhanced the Boston Museum of Fine Arts in his native city. The Warren Cup is now in the British Museum.

Like Gill's guild, the brotherhood had an underlying philosophy – Greek ideals and high-minded aestheticism. At the height of its fame, six men lived in the house. It was furnished with fine examples of antique furniture, Oriental carpets and rugs, tapestries, primitive paintings and rare books, while Warren's vast collection of vases, bronzes, ivories and other priceless antiquities were on show. The residents kept Arabian horses and there were St Bernard dogs, good food and a well-stocked cellar.

Lewes House, School Hill. (Paul Lantsbury)

The garden of Lewes House, Church Lane. (Paul Lantsbury)

William Rothenstein, the painter who introduced Warren to Auguste Rodin, described Lewes House as 'a monkish establishment where women were not welcomed'.

George Justice, the old established Lewes firm of furniture restorers that still exists in Market Street, is believed to have installed the staircase, panelling and fixtures in the annexe to Lewes House, a former stables used by Warren as a study, which he called Thebes. His extensive circle of friends, whom he entertained frequently, reflected his interest in the arts.

In 1928, Lewes House and other properties, including School Hill House, were given by Warren to H. Asa Thomas, who had begun as Warren's secretary and became his friend and business associate.

When he returned from Rome later that year, serious illness caused Warren to undergo surgery and he died in a London nursing home on 28 December 1928. His ashes were taken to Bagni di Lucca in Italy where they were placed with Marshall's remains in the English Cemetery. They rest beneath a simple monument topped appropriately with a Grecian urn.

Warren left an estate plagued by legal problems. A total of 240 items of his furniture fetched $38,885 at auction. His will set up the E. P. Warren Praelector at Corpus Christi College, Oxford, but stipulated that the holder should live in or near the college and teach only men. The conditions were not maintained.

A bronze statuette, purchased from Warren in 1904 by the Boston Museum of Fine Arts, was returned to a French Museum after it was determined to have been stolen in 1901.

Since 1974, the Grade II-listed Lewes House has been the offices of Lewes District Council. The principal rooms – the Business Room, Red Drawing Room, Hepplewhite Bedroom and Dining Room – remain in their original state.

'Thebes' was Edward Perry Warren's studio in the twitten next to Lewes House, where he stored 'The Kiss'. (Paul Lantsbury)

DID YOU KNOW?

In 1900, the wealthy expatriate Edward Perry Warren, founder of the Lewes House Brotherhood, commissioned Auguste Rodin to create a version of *The Kiss* for £1,000. The statue arrived in the town in 1904 and Warren placed it in Thebes, his study. The statue is one of three executed by Rodin, is larger than the original, and is generally considered to be the best.

In 1914 Warren arranged for the statue to be exhibited at the Town Hall, with the intention of donating it to the town. It was placed in a corner of the Assembly Room but very soon there was a campaign, firstly to have it covered and then to have it removed. Concerns were raised that its content and nakedness would affect soldiers who were billeted in Lewes during the First World War. In 1917 it was returned to Thebes and placed under a tarpaulin until Warren died in 1928. Lewes House and its contents were auctioned in 1929 but Rodin's work failed to reach its reserve price. What could have been perhaps Lewes' most distinguished work of art was purchased by the Art Fund and a public appeal for the Tate Gallery in 1953. The gallery's director, Sir John Rothenstein, was the son of the man who had first introduced Warren to Rodin. The statue came back to Lewes temporarily in 1999 as part of the Millennium celebrations and Thebes was briefly turned into an art gallery.

7. Matters of Faith: Lewes and Religion

Lewes, like many towns and cities, is a place of many faiths and varied religious buildings. However, it has been visited with more religious turmoil and controversy than is perhaps expected in a town of its size.

The Priory of St Pancras

It is difficult now for the visitor, strolling amid the picturesque ruins of the Priory of St Pancras, to picture easily the community that once existed here. Richly endowed by its founders and their successors with land tithes and fishing rights, it had a great church, a chapter house, lodgings, chapels, farms, an infirmary, workshops and outbuildings. It had its own masons' yard and manufactured decorated glazed floor tiles, while there was a school of sacred painting that worked throughout Sussex (surviving figurative carvings are displayed in the British Museum). Dozens of monks and lay brothers, along with visitors, lived, worked, prayed and worshipped here for four and a half centuries. William de Warenne, 2nd Earl of Surrey and son of William and Gundrada, the founders, gave nine Lewes churches to the priory, and as many again in Sussex and many others elsewhere.

Indeed, that vanished life is given added poignancy with the knowledge that this was not only one of the largest monastic houses in the country, a rival to the better-known abbeys of Rievaulx, Whitby and Fountains in Yorkshire, but it was the first Cluniac house in England, founded for the French order, which is a reformed version of the Benedictines.

Bounded by today's Cockshut Road and Priory Street, the precinct was at least the same extent as the area covered by the then walled town of Lewes on the ridge to the north. A hospice for the priory was built in the twelfth century and stood west of the priory gate, but today all that remains is one wall with the thirteenth-century multi-shafted jamb of an arch.

In the thirteenth century the hospice became St John the Baptist, the parish church for the surrounding area, which survived the Dissolution of the Monasteries. In Southover High Street, opposite Southover Grange, is a small, square building. It is the chapel, all that remains of the Hospital of St James, which was founded by William de Warenne, 2nd Earl of Surrey, for (as a plaque states) twenty-four elderly or infirm brothers and sisters and for pilgrims and the sick. It was maintained by Lewes Priory and survived the Dissolution of the Monasteries.

But all was not tranquil in the monastic years. The priory was founded between 1078 and 1082, in the reign of Cluniac pope Gregory VII. Before embarking on a pilgrimage to Rome, William and Gundrada had determined to build a priory in Lewes, which they owned thanks to the rape and possession of the town by the Normans. On returning from Rome, having stayed at the great Abbey of St Peter and St Paul at

Chapel of the former hospital of St James, Southover High Street. (Terry Philpot)

Part of the ruins of the Priory of St Pancras. (Terry Philpot)

Cluny, and so taken by the standards of religious life which they had observed there, they determined that Lewes' foundation would be Cluniac. Its first prior came from France with three monks. The name St Pancras derived from a shrine on the site dedicated to the Roman boy martyr.

However, Henry III installed his forces in the precinct in 1264, during the Battle of Lewes, as they (unsuccessfully) resisted the attack from Simon de Montfort.

But far worse was to come. It was Thomas Cromwell, Henry's Chancellor, who is responsible for what we see today. In 1535 Richard Layton, the king and Cromwell's principal agent in the Dissolution of the Monasteries – 'the king's faithful dog' as the *Victoria County History* of *Sussex* calls him – reported to Cromwell the 'corruption' and 'treason' that he found at the priory (but then he found it wherever he went). Lewes survived a couple of years, harassed, but Cromwell was steadfast in executing his monarch's wishes in dissolving the monasteries. In November 1537 the priory, with the 2,000 acres of land it owned in Sussex, came into the Crown's possession. The remaining twenty-three monks and eighty servants were sent away with small pensions and gratuities.

Cromwell engaged an Italian engineer to lead a demolition team. They went to work with such thoroughness and dispatch that by the next year Cromwell could come into ownership of the manor of Southover and the site of the dissolved monastery. Here he built a substantial house where the prior's lodgings had once stood and whether from piety or mockery called it The Lord's Place. When, in his turn, he got on the wrong side of Henry, the property went to Anne of Cleves and after her death to the earls of Dorset.

In the 1830s residential development took place, cutting into the priory burial grounds, and the builders sold bones, teeth and skulls they found when digging the foundations.

The new railway from Lewes to Brighton made its own destructive mark, cutting in to the foundations of the chapter house and church apse and exposing the foundations and burials including those of William.

William's grave was discovered in 1845 when the railway was being constructed, but Gundrada's remains had been moved to St Margaret's, Isfield, after the dissolution and then in 1775 to St John the Baptist next to the priory site. In 1847 William was reburied next to her, and they rest in the church's south chapel under the original black-marble tombstone from the priory, carved to the memory of Gundrada, that had been incorporated into a Tudor period memorial to an Edward Shurley in St Margaret's Church.

The present day has not always been mindful of the richness of its heritage. Precinct walls have been demolished for housing development and a car park.

The anchorites of Lewes

St Anne's Church, originally known as St Mary Westout, dates from around 1160 and was part of the endowment given to the Cluniac priory of St Pancras. Its oldest parts are the tower, the nave and the south chapel, built in the early twelfth century, although the Victorians did extensive alterations to the exterior of the nave. There is also a beamed ceiling from the fourteenth century.

The antiquity of the church, in Western Road, is further enhanced by a very unusual feature: this is a rare thirteenth-century anchoress's cell. Anchorites are often confused

Above: The Church of St John-sub-Castro, Abinger Place. (Paul Lantsbury)

Right: St Anne's Church was home to an anchoress in the thirteenth century.

Wall memorial to Prince Magnus, the anchorite, on the external south wall of the Church of St John-sub-Castro, Abinger Place. (Terry Philpot)

with hermits. But while both withdraw from the world and live a solitary life of prayer (as opposed to the communal one of the monk or nun), unlike hermits, anchorites must take a vow of stability of place, which means they are permanently enclosed in cells attached to churches. Also unlike hermits, anchorites are subject to a religious rite of consecration that closely resembles the funeral rite, following which – theoretically, at least – they would be considered dead to the world. Anchorites are answerable only to a bishop.

This cell is on the site of the vestry. St Richard de Wyche, Bishop of Chichester, left five shillings in 1253 to whoever fulfilled this role. It is believed that he was interested in anchorites to the extent that he may even have written a book of guidance for them. The woman (an anchoress) who inhabited the cell allowed herself to be walled up and it is thought that bones found on the site of the cell were hers. They were reinterred in the chancel.

Unusual as this may be, Lewes, in fact, was home to another anchorite. He was Prince Magnus, wrongly supposed son of Harold II, whose cell was also here probably in the twelfth century. It is uncertain where the cell would have been in the original Saxon church, but it may have been built onto the side of the chancel, perhaps with a squint (a narrow opening) to view the altar.

The present church of St John-sub-Castro, Abinger Place, which was built in 1839 on the site of an eleventh-century church of the same name, has a tablet set into the outside wall, through the gates and on the left. It bears a commemorative inscription, which in Latin reads, 'Intombed [sic] a soldier here of royal race, Magnus his name, from mighty Danish source, resigned his title, gave the lamb his place, and closed as lonely eremite his course.' One authority says of Magnus that 'becoming disgusted with the world and all earthly things, the vanity and vexation of which his own unhappy experience had taught him retired from society and became an anchorite'.

The Protestant Martyrs
The seventeen Protestant Martyrs, victims of what are known as the Marian Persecutions, are, with Tom Paine, the most well-known characters in Lewes' history.

When Mary Tudor, eldest child daughter of Henry VIII, succeeded her half-brother, Edward VI, in July 1853, she sought to reintroduce Catholicism and as a result 288 Protestants were executed for 'heresy'. Seventeen of those executed were burned at the stake in Lewes outside the Old Star Inn, where the Town Hall now stands in the High Street – hence, her name, 'Bloody Mary'. There was no discrimination in who she executed: from pregnant women to scholars, the poor to Thomas Cranmer, Archbishop of Canterbury.

The first of the seventeen was Dutchman Deryk Carver, a brewer in the village of Brighthelmston (now Brighton). A Flemish Protestant born around 1505, he fled religious persecution in his home country to settle in the village in the 1540s and purchased the Black Lion Brewery, a replica of which stands in Black Lion Street, Brighton. Carver became a wealthy member of the community.

In 1554 he was arrested at his home while praying with eleven others, three of whom were also arrested and eventually executed. He was tried in London in 1555. At his trial he refused to recant his Protestantism and then attacked the Catholic faith as 'poison and sorcery ... Your ceremonies in the Church be beggary and poison'. He was found guilty and burnt at the stake in Lewes on 22 July 1555. His profession was mocked by his being placed in a barrel before he was executed.

On 6 June 1556, four more Protestants died in Lewes at the stake: Thomas Harland, John Oswold, Thomas Avington and Thomas Reed. Two weeks later, two more were put to death: Thomas Wood and Thomas Miles. Finally, on around the 22 June, ten more died: Richard Woodman, George Stevens, William Mainard, Alexander Hosman, Thomasina Wood, Margery Morris and her son James, Denis Burcis, Ann Ashdon (a resident of Lewes) and Mary Groves.

A memorial obelisk to the martyrs was erected on Cliffe Hill in 1901 at a cost of £900. A plaque is on the wall of the Town Hall, in whose undercroft the martyrs were held.

Plaque to the Protestant martyrs outside the Town Hall, High Street. (Paul Lantsbury)

DID YOU KNOW?

While Lewes' bonfire night is usually taken to be the traditional commemoration of the Gunpowder Plot, it is alone in burning an effigy of a generic pope and remembering the seventeen Lewes Protestant Martyrs burned in the marketplace for their faith. In the past, effigies of Pope Paul V, Pius IX and Leo XIII have been burned, as have, more recently, those of the Archbishop of Canterbury and the then Liberal Democrat leader and deputy Prime Minister Nick Clegg, while the use of holy water has been mocked. 'No popery' banners have been displayed and the Revd Ian Paisley once visited.

There appear to have been similar commemorations in the town at the end of the reign of Mary Tudor, who was responsible for the martyrs' deaths, but the first bonfire wasn't recorded until 1679. There are five bonfire societies, each with its own territory, and tens of thousands of people attend.

Another plaque is on the wall of the Eastgate Baptist Church, though this site and building has no connection with the events. A large tablet stands in the south wall of the graveyard next to the parish Church of St Mary the Virgin, Warbleton, 18 miles east of Lewes. This reads, 'Close by, on the meadow behind, stood the abode of Richard Woodman, farmer and ironmaster. Burnt at Lewes, 22 June, 1557.'

Bishop Richard Challoner

It is an historical irony that the town which, in some ways, is best known for having a Guy Fawkes' Night, with its strongly anti-Catholic hue and memorial to the seventeen Protestant Martyrs, is also the birthplace of Bishop Richard Challoner, Catholic priest and religious writer.

But Challoner's Catholic credentials were somewhat unusual for his time. He was born in Lewes on 29 September 1691. His father, also Richard, was a Presbyterian wine-barrel maker and after his death his mother, Grace (nee Willard) from Ringer, was reduced to poverty and became housekeeper to the Catholic Gage family, 5 miles to the south-east at Firle Place. She may have been a Catholic, although that is not known for certain, or she may have become one under the influence of her employers. But Challoner was raised in the faith, though not baptised until he was around thirteen, at Warkworth, Northamptonshire, home of the recusant Catholic family of George Holman, where his mother was by then in service.

At Warkworth, the chaplain John Gother recommended him for education to the priesthood at the English College at Douai in France where he studied from 1705 to 1708. He was ordained in 1716, having in between times held academic posts and taking further degrees.

In 1724 he published the first of more than sixty books, and while he blossomed as a writer, he is less well known for his originality than for popularising mainstream Douai tradition. His books challenged both Protestants and atheists, and he wrote on meditation, marianology and apologetics. He is best known today for his revision of the Douai-Rheims Bible, which was the standard work for Catholics into the mid-twentieth century.

His pastoral side was expressed in his ministry to the poor of London, to which he came in 1730 and was vicar-general to the London district with the care of 25,000 Catholics.

When it seemed he would succeed to be Bishop of London, he objected on the grounds that he had been brought up an Anglican (this may suggest that his mother was not a Catholic) but papal dispensation was given.

He lived austerely, acted as almoner to the 9th Duke of Norfolk, founded a school (and many Catholic schools today bear his name) and, though he was not himself a Jesuit, he resisted the secular clergy taking over the Jesuits' college at St Omer.

Challoner was lucky to escape from his London house in Gloucester Street, Queen Square, when the anti-Catholic Gordon Riots of 1780 broke out and the London mob, whipped up by the mad Scot, Lord George Gordon, burned and pillaged Catholic chapels, houses, and businesses. Challoner found sanctuary in the house of his friend, the woollen merchant William Mawhood, in Finchley.

The effect of this and his distress at the destruction of homes and chapels where he had said mass for fifty years probably led to the stroke in January 1781 that killed him at his home. His last word was 'charity', and he indicated to his chaplain Joseph Bolton his pocket containing money for the poor. He was buried, with both Anglican and Catholic rites, at Milton in Berkshire. In 1946 his remains were exhumed and reburied in Westminster Cathedral.

St Thomas à Becket Church

It seems undoubtedly the case that this church was built in Cliffe High Street to honour the murdered saint of Canterbury. Now Anglican, it first stood as a chapel for Cliffe, in South Malling parish, probably in the twelfth century. Reconstructed in the fourteenth century, much of what one sees today is the result of Victorian restoration.

St Thomas à Becket Church, Cliffe High Street.
(Paul Lantsbury)

There's an attractive legend that appears to underscore the Becket link, which is that the four barons who brutally murdered him in Canterbury Cathedral fled to South Malling. Alas, for Lewes and the church, this has never been verified. Indeed, Richard Winston, Becket's biographer, makes the claim that the knights headed north and sought refuge in the castle where Hugh de Moreville was constable. The far surer local link to Becket is that he held the manor of South Malling.

Notes of Dissent

Religion of a different stripe from the extravagance of the priory's Cluniac worship, Catholicism and High Anglicanism came in the form of the long history of dissent and nonconformity enjoyed in Lewes. This was once perhaps most impressively represented by the Independent Congregational Tabernacle, which stood where the undistinguished Cliffe High Street precinct now stands. It is difficult to imagine now that this place, with its four-column entrance, built in 1813, rebuilt in 1832 and demolished in 1954, should have accommodated 1,200 worshippers, while 500 children could be taken by its Sunday school.

Henry Acton

Unitarianism, with its rejection of the divine nature of Christ, is perhaps, with Quakerism, the most dissident of all dissenting churches and Acton, a Unitarian minister, born in Lewes on 10 March 1797, was one of its foremost advocates.

The third of four sons of William Acton, a labourer, and his wife Mary, he became a printer's apprentice when he was sixteen. Through Bible study he moved from Anglicanism to Unitarianism. This led him to the General Baptist Chapel in Eastport Lane. He so impressed those whom he met in a discussion group that when his apprenticeship ended in 1818, members of the Unitarian congregation of Westgate Chapel in the High Street offered to subsidise his attendance at a Hove school run by Dr John Morell, a Unitarian minister.

That same year, with another apprentice, Acton had begun to supply the pulpit at the Old Meeting House in Ditchling nearby to Lewes. This he alternated with services at Eastport Lane. The end of his education in 1821 saw him appointed minister at Walthamstow, Essex, and two years later he was made co-pastor with James Manning (1754–1831) at George's Meeting, Exeter. He made Exeter his home, marrying and becoming father of three sons and three daughters, founding the journal *The Gospel Advocate* and school teaching.

But when Manning died in 1831, Acton's wish to be appointed sole pastor was rejected by the congregation, who appointed a second minister. This may have been due to Acton's reluctance for pastoral work.

Some found Acton haughty and his raillery could cause offence, but he was exceptional as a preacher and as an advocate for Unitarianism, even at one time besting the bishop of Exeter in debate. He was also active in civil rights and liberal causes. He died in 1843.

Westgate Chapel and Bull House

While Acton today would not recognise the interior of the Westgate Chapel, at No. 82a High Street, it remains a Unitarian meeting house. However, while there appears to be no obvious connection between chapel and house, other than their being adjacent to one another, their histories are, in fact, intimately intertwined and cannot be considered separately.

One hundred years before Acton was there, Tom Paine had known the chapel, which was then Presbyterian, as his parents-in-law were attenders. A stone wall in the basement may probably date from the first Norman defensive wall built as part of the West Gate. It also has a Tudor door, Elizabethan hand-made bricks and huge beams, which survived the extensive works undertaken in the creation of the chapel from part of Bull House between 1698 and 1700 by two clergymen – Revd Thomas Barnard, a Presbyterian from Glyndebourne, and Revd Edward Newton, formerly of St Mary's Westout (now St Anne's Church, Western Road). Both had fallen foul of the laws which sought conformity to the doctrine of the Church of England. (A tablet commemorates them and other expelled

Westgate Chapel, High Street. (Paul Lantsbury)

Westgate Chapel interior.

clergy.) It was Barnard who actually bought the Bull Inn for £210 and this marks the greatest change in Bull House's history, as it was split in two, creating two separate and very different properties.

Until then, Bull Inn or Bull House had been a medieval hall house and inn inside the town's West Gate, which was demolished in 1763. The oldest surviving work dates from the fifteenth century.

Sir Henry Goring bought the house in 1583 for £160 from Thomas Matthew. The new owner pulled down the back part and replaced it with a flint and stone extension. The belief is that the inn remained at the front and Goring's town house at the back, but there is no architectural evidence to support this and his work may only have been to extend the inn. A fatal stabbing during a brawl occurred in the inn in 1594. Goring's son Edward sold Bull House to Edward Claggett of Portslade in 1612, who, three years later, sold it to Thomas Oliver, a merchant, for £325. In 1655 it is recorded that a Cavalier and a Roundhead engaged in another brawl at the inn. The inn was let to tenants until sold to Thomas Adams in 1698, who quickly disposed of it that same year to Barnard.

By 1700 Westgate Chapel had been built, for which the south part of the building was gutted, and became a recognised, that is, a legal, place of worship for nonconformists. In 1719 Barnard sold Bull House for £100 to the Revd John Ollive, minister of the chapel from 1711 to 1740. His son was Samuel, a tobacconist, and he gave lodgings there to Thomas Paine.

Since 1774, when the Ollive business, then partly run by Paine, collapsed, Bull House has housed several businesses, including an ironmongery and a restaurant. In 1922 Alderman John Every, a Unitarian and owner of the Phoenix ironworks, commissioned a renovation of Bull House by the architect, conservationist and antiquarian Walter Godfrey. Every presented the building to the Sussex Archeological Society, whose home it has been since 1936.

Bull House, High Street. (Paul Lantsbury)

Until Barnard made his £210 investment, with whatever further costs he and Newton were to incur, the chapel's congregation had a strong links to St Michael's Church, which stands across the street. Here the incumbent was the young Revd Walter Postlethwaite, a contemporary of Newton at Emmanuel College, Cambridge, and a Fifth Monarchist. (The millenarianist Fifth Monarchists were one of many radical Christian groups that flourished during the rule of Cromwell.)

Two congregations appeared to share the chapel but then split, with one taking itself off to a smaller chapel in Eastport Lane; around 1760 the two reunited. Those who had been in Eastport Lane sold the stone from their chapel and the wood was used to create the present vestry of Westgate Chapel, which stands above the old stable yard at the rear of the chapel.

Westgate Chapel had an impressive Georgian structure to allow for an open space for nonconformist worship. But in 1840 there was a radical restyling, and in 1913

Gargoyles on Bull House. (Paul Lantsbury)

DID YOU KNOW?

The gargoyles (in fact, satyrs) on Bull House helped give it the nickname 'the monkey house'. They date from the time of Sir Henry Goring's extension to the property in the sixteenth century.

restructuring took place again (paid for by John Every) to create a look more in keeping with an Anglican church. Stained-glass windows, installed in 1924, moved the chapel further to greater decoration.

Cost has precluded a wholesale restoration to the now-preferred Regency structure but, at the time of writing, decoration in more Georgian style is taking place, while the original Georgian pulpit, its sounding board and its marquetry will be restored – it was damaged and used as a table top for many years and will now be displayed below where the north-facing pulpit once was.

Bull House and the Westgate Chapel share a history that joins political and theological dissent, which would hardly be guessed at by most passers-by.

Jireh Chapel

There were several evangelical chapels in the town, some of a strong Calvinist tenor. Because of its founder, one of the most notable was an Independent Chapel, now gone, founded by Selina, Countess of Huntingdon, who had been inspired by John and Charles Wesley and built her first chapel for her eponymous 'Connexion' in Brighton.

However, the Jireh Chapel is an offshoot of the countess's endeavours. The American Colonial-style building dates to 1805 and was much enlarged in 1826, and, with its Sunday school, is one of the few Grade I-listed buildings in Lewes and the surrounding area. It is also only one of seven Free Presbyterian chapels in England.

The Jireh Chapel, Malling Street.
(Terry Philpot)

DID YOU KNOW?

The red mechanical tiles facing the Jireh Chapel are said to be the greatest expanse of such tiles in the town.

The building, at No. 26 Malling Street, is constructed of red mathematical tiles and grey slate, hung on a wooden frame, with chequered brickwork in places. There are galleries on three sides, box-pews and a central pulpit behind the table at the west end. All this and the wooden interior afford a true flavour of nonconformist worship. It was restored to its original form in the latter part of the 1990s.

William Huntingdon, who combined coal heaving with evangelism, rests in the churchyard. He insisted on having SS for 'saved sinner' affixed to his name. He died in Tunbridge Wells in 1813 having married into the aristocracy. The funeral procession, said to be a mile long, brought him back to Lewes in a hearse drawn by black-plumed horses.

Quaker Meeting House

The Quaker meeting house in Friars Walk is not the original one. In 1655 Thomas Robinson 'Declared the Truth' at The Croft, the home of John Russell, at what is now No. 43 Southover Street. It was later that year in that house that George Fox, founder of the Society of Friends (the Quakers' formal name), and Alexander Parker came from Steyning to a meeting.

Quaker meeting house, Friary Walk. (Paul Lantsbury)

There was still no meeting house and for several years the Friends met in one another's homes or, on occasion, held public meetings. But under the Act of Uniformity of 1662, the Anglican Church's rites, sacraments, ministry and prayers were established and this was complemented by the Conventicle Act of 1664, which forbade worship by any group of more than five people not in the same household, thus effectively making illegal any worship other than Anglican. The Act of Toleration of 1688 allowed some dissenting worship if an oath was sworn, but Quakers do not swear oaths. They were fined or imprisoned for holding meetings, refusing to pay tithes and refusing to attend Anglican church services.

The first Quaker meeting house was opened in 1675, around 100 yards from the present meeting house. This may have been an ordinary house where walls between some rooms had been removed to create more space. Jane Kidder was appointed to live in the house because although the law allowed for the demolition of illegal places of worship, her habitation made the meeting house a dwelling place.

The first record of a burial at Friars Walk occurs in 1697, although a deed, with a 1,000-year lease, for a burial place was signed in 1674.

In October 1783, a sale for £110 was sought and in November the Friends vacated the property when the Particular Baptists temporarily took over. The present Quaker meeting house was built and opened in June 1784 at a cost of £229.8s.6d. Within twenty years, and then another ten years later, enlargement was required to cope with numbers. While the interior has not changed markedly, the exterior has been several times extended.

St Pancras Catholic Church

Another religious group that suffered persecution and exclusion, even into the lifetimes of our great-great-grandparents, were Roman Catholics. When Catholic worship

St Pancras Church, Western Road.

eventually became lawful, mass was said at No. 10 Priory Crescent, appropriately near the ruins of the priory. In 1870 the Church of St Pancras was built. Where the present forecourt of the church now stands at Irelands Lane was the parish school, which replaced two cottages.

The first parish priest was Fr Hubert Wood, whose parents paid for the buildings and the furnishings, while his mother made some of the vestments still used today.

When, in 1930, St Pancras Primary School was opened in De Montfort Road, Irelands Lane became available for development and the church was demolished, and in 1939 the present church was built at a cost of £7,500. The stained-glass windows come from the original church.

8. Crime and Punishment

Unusually for a town of its size, Lewes has been home to two prisons, and now has a third one.

Lewes Naval Prison
Lewes Naval Prison was opened in 1793 in North Street as the Lewes House of Correction. It was enlarged in 1817 and sold to the Admiralty in 1853. It was demolished in 1963. A part of a wall can still be seen in Lancaster Street, where a plaque speaks of the prison's origin as the Lewes House of Correction and the fact that 'Russian' prisoners of war later served time there.

The reference to 'Russian' prisoners concerns some of the prison's most historically interesting inmates. They were, in fact, the 100 Swedish-speaking Finnish prisoners who had fought with Russia during the Crimean War. After their release the officers wrote to the senior constable thanking him for the way they had been treated.

However, conditions were not so wonderful that some didn't want to get out, and in 1855 three Finns had escaped and were recaptured in late March. A fourth escaped in April. He was found in the King's Arms drinking half a pint of rum. He was returned to the prison and placed in solitary confinement with only bread and water to eat and drink.

Obelisk in churchyard of St John-sub-Castro, Abinger Place, where the 'Russian' prisoners of war are buried. (Paul Lantsbury)

Plaque where Lewes Naval Prison stood in Lancaster Street, commemorating the 'Russian' prisoners. (Terry Philpot)

Lewes Prison staff, including female warders, 1912. (Courtesy of Bob Cairns)

A popular Finnish folk song, 'Oolannin sota' (Crimean War), which tells of the prisoners' capture and incarceration in Lewes, is thought to have been written by one of the Lewes prisoners in captivity.

It may seem curious, though, that a town with no connection to the Royal Navy should contain a naval prison. However, before Lewes and Bodmin were built, the civilian prisons of Maidstone, Winchester and Exeter were used to incarcerate naval personnel, but the Navy had no control over the prisons. The Admiralty favoured Lewes as a site for a prison as it was around equal distance between Chatham and Portsmouth, the two largest ports, and so the Admiralty bought the House of Correction in 1853.

Apart from a part of a wall and the plaque, there remains another physical reminder of the prison's history. Twenty-eight of the Finnish prisoners died in Lewes, many of tuberculosis. Their comrades erected a simple headstone over the burial plot in the churchyard of St John-sub-Castro, Abinger Place. This was replaced in 1877 with an impressive obelisk commissioned by Tsar Alexander II, with the names of the prisoners engraved on it. In 1957 it was refurbished by the Soviet government and in 1985 received Grade II listing.

However, the memorial fell into disrepair, the cross at the top was broken and the names became difficult to decipher. In 2013 the Russian and Finnish ambassadors attended an unveiling of the refurbished memorial, paid for by funds from their two countries and the UK.

One of the panels reproduces the wording of the first memorial:

> Soon will the Lord come
> who has said
> Those that on me believe
> them will I
> Raise to Eternal Life

Lewes Prison
Law and order in Lewes is symbolised by the law courts and Lewes Prison, built in 1853. Today, the prison is a local one, holding convicted and remanded adult males mainly from East Sussex and West Sussex courts.

Lewes Crown Court
Lewes Crown Court in the High Street now houses the Lewes Combined Court Centre, which it shares with Lewes County Court. The building was originally the county hall, designed by John Johnson. It was built between 1808 and 1812. Many well-known trials have been held here. In earlier times, many of those held temporarily in the Brighton police cells (now the Old Police Cells Museum under what was Brighton Town Hall) were either tried at the Lewes Crown Court or hanged at Lewes Prison. In its more distant past, like that of the prison and law courts, it has featured some of the more notorious cases recorded in the annals of criminal history. These five are worth noting:

Lewes Crown Court, the former county hall, which is shared with the Lewes County Court, High Street. (Paul Lantsbury)

John Lawrence

Many murderers are known for their crime. John Lawrence is better known for his victim, Chief Constable Henry Solomon, Brighton's second chief officer (now chief constable) in 1832. It was notable also because Soloman was a Jew. Lawrence was tried at Lewes, found guilty and hanged at Horsham Prison, the last person to be executed there.

Solomon was interviewing John Lawrence, aged twenty-three, in Brighton police station about the theft of a roll of carpet. The prisoner became agitated and struck Solomon with a poker. Solomon was taken to his home to be treated but died there afterwards. Solomon is believed to be the only chief constable ever to be murdered on duty.

Percy Lefroy Mapleton

Percy Lefroy Mapleton, the so-called 'railway murderer', was hanged at Lewes on 29 November 1881, having been tried at Maidstone. His executioner was the renowned hangman William Marwood. It was the first case where the police had used a composite picture for a wanted appeal in a newspaper.

Mapleton was only twenty-one when he murdered sixty-four-year-old Isaac Frederick Gold, a coin dealer returning by train from London Bridge to his home in Brighton. Seen disembarking at Preston Park Station covered in blood, Mapleton claimed to have been attacked by two men. He was taken by train to Brighton where he was questioned by the police. He was released and taken by a police officer to a relative's home in Wallington, Surrey. However, when news that a search in the tunnel at Balcombe had found Gold's body, revealing that he had been shot, Mapleton escaped from the officer in Wallington and disappeared. He was later found, under an assumed name, in Stepney, London.

Mapleton was allowed to wear full evening dress at his trial in the belief it would impress the jury. It didn't. They retired for only ten minutes to bring in a guilty verdict. Awaiting execution he confessed to the murder of a soldier but later withdrew the statement.

In the twentieth century, Lewes saw the trials of three of the most notorious murderers of modern times: Sydney Harry Fox, who committed matricide; George Haigh, the so-called 'acid bath murderer'; and Dr John Bodkin Adams, though he was actually acquitted of the murder for which he was tried.

Sydney Harry Fox

Matricide is an unusual crime and Sidney Harry Fox was a petty criminal, engaging in forgery and theft before he hit the headlines in 1930 when he murdered his mother, Florence. They had lived a poverty-stricken existence and he had persuaded her to take out life insurance for accidental death. He strangled her in a hotel in Margate, a fact discovered only after her body was exhumed as the original belief had been that she had died of suffocation in a fire at the hotel. He was tried at Lewes and hanged at Maidstone Prison.

George Haigh

Haigh, who was tried at Lewes but hanged at Wandsworth Prison by executioner Albert Pierrepoint on 10 August 1949, killed six people but claimed to have killed nine. It emerged during the investigation that he had misunderstood the term *corpus delicti* and believed that if there was no body, then a murder conviction could not be made. Thus, he disposed of his victims' bodies by immersing them in baths of concentrated sulphuric acid. But there was enough forensic evidence to secure a conviction.

The counsel for the trial and the judge were particularly distinguished. Sir Hartley (later Lord) Shawcross, former Nuremburg prosecutor and attorney-general in the post-war Labour government, successfully urged the jury to reject Haigh's plea of insanity. Sir David Maxwell-Fife, as Lord Dilhorne, later Lord Chancellor in Conservative governments, defended Haigh. They sat before Sir Travers Humphreys, a veteran of many trials, who had successfully prosecuted Horatio Bottomley and heard the appeal against his conviction of William Joyce (Lord Haw Haw).

Dr John Bodkin Adams

Adams was an Eastbourne GP charged with the murder of a patient after more than 160 of his female patients died between 1946 and 1956, and he had benefited under the wills of 132 of them. His committal trial was heard at Lewes.

Adams was found not guilty at his sensational Old Bailey trial, coverage of which was shown around the world. There were later claims of government interference influencing its outcome. However, he returned to Lewes in 1957, where he was found guilty of thirteen offences of prescription fraud, lying on cremation forms, obstructing a police search, and failing to keep a dangerous drugs register. He was fined £2,400 plus costs of £457. Having resigned from the NHS before the trial, he was later struck off the medical register, but was reinstated four years later. It is now widely believed that Adams was, in fact, a serial murderer.

9. 'Gainst All Disasters: Tragedies Strike Lewes

For a town that is, to all appearances, calm and largely unchanging, Lewes has been visited by three particularly notable disasters.

The Lewes Avalanche

The first disaster was one more to be expected in the Swiss Alps than in a small town set amid the undulating, gentle hills of the South Downs – an avalanche.

At Christmas in 1836 Lewes experienced the only avalanche in the world ever to occur at sea level. The severe winter across the whole country began at the end of October 1836 and lasted until April the following year, with the south-east particularly affected. It was some of the worst weather on record – gale-force winds combined with freezing temperatures and heavy snow. On Christmas Eve, a large storm joined the already high winds and snow to produce massive blizzard and great snow drifts; in Lewes the drifts were said to be 20 feet high.

By Christmas night a 20-foot-deep overhanging ledge of snow had built on the sheer edge of Cliffe Hill, buffeted by a north-easterly blizzard. The most immediate danger was to Boulder Row, seven terraced labourers' cottages for the poor, in South Street, owned by South Malling parish. The cottagers were urged to leave their homes until the snow had melted but they refused. On Boxing Day an intimation of what was to come occurred when snow from the clifftop fell and swept a timber yard into the River Ouse.

What had been feared was soon to follow when, at 10.15 the following morning, the mass of snow fell onto the cottages, and while exactly how many people were in them at the time is not known, contemporary reports claimed it was fifteen.

The cottages were not just crushed. Such was the force and weight of the fall that they were swept along the road, a white heap of snow the only marker to where people had once lived. *The Sussex Weekly Advertiser* reported: 'The mass appeared to strike the houses at the base, heaving them upwards, and then breaking over them like a gigantic wave. There was nothing but a mound of white snow.'

The rescue took seven hours and seven people were saved. Eight died of hypothermia and suffocation. The printed cotton dress, worn by two-year-old Fanny Boakes, believed to be the granddaughter of another survivor, Fanny Sherlock, is held by the Anne of Cleves House museum. The contemporary painting of the event, attributed to Thomas Henwood, hangs there.

Today, the victims lie in a common grave with no marker in the churchyard of St Michael the Archangel at South Malling, although the public raised money for a memorial tablet on the north wall of the church, and a fund was also set up to assist those who had survived.

Snowdrop Inn, South Street, which stands on the spot of the poor labourers' cottages. These were destroyed in the Lewes avalanche of 1836, which killed fifteen people. (Stephen McKay)

The most obvious reminder of the disaster is a public house erected on the site of Boulder Row. In contrast to the horrors that occurred, the pub bears an elegant, gentle and calming name – the Snowdrop Inn.

The Great Fire of Lewes

The so-called 'Great Fire of Lewes', which took place in the early morning of Tuesday 4 October 1904, destroyed Dusart's in the High Street and also severely damaged neighbouring properties. There have been other fires in Lewes but none so extensive or spectacular. Now the site of A & Y Cumming and Lewesiana, Dusart's was a tobacconist, toy shop, stationer, hairdresser and offered hot and cold baths.

At two o'clock that morning, fruiterer and greengrocer George Turner, of New Road, was on his way to Brighton market when he saw flames in the establishment owned by Frank Dusart. Shouting 'fire!' and failing to rouse whoever was inside, he ran to the police station, where he told Sgt Smith, who then alerted the fire brigade. The brigade owned manual engines, which the *Sussex Express* described as 'unequal to the task' and 'antiquated'.

Neighbours, including a local doctor, took part in the rescue attempts, which had to be made from the back of the building. Horses and carriages were removed from nearby stables.

There were no casualties, although at one time it was feared that the ten-year-old son of the owner had perished, but it was then found that he had escaped by jumping from a window after saving a younger brother and his mother.

Dusants, in the High Street, with (inset), the fire that destroyed it in 1904. (Courtesy of Bob Cairns)

The new fire station opened in 1907 at the bottom of North Street after the 'Great Fire of Lewes'. (Courtesy of Bob Cairns)

The Great Fire highlighted the inadequacy of the fire brigade and the council was subject to much criticism by press and public. The town had had two fire services. The Lewes Fire Establishment was created in 1842 and was staffed by two directors and twenty firefighters, who were assisted the next year by a manual fire engine purchased through public subscription. But in 1844 the Cliffe Volunteer Fire Brigade came into being, with a fire station in Cliffe Square where a new fire engine was also housed. After the borough was incorporated in 1881, the two services were merged. Like its predecessors, this was a service of local volunteers, but in 1889 a motion put before the council to consider a salaried fire service was defeated.

The only modern appliances used at the conflagration had come from the Brighton Volunteer and Police Fire Brigades. Following the fire, a new fire station was built in 1907 in North Street, where a new steam fire engine was kept. A fire brigade committee was formed by the council and the borough surveyor took on the role of chief fire officer.

The Lewes Floods

A town set on the banks of the river is likely to be in danger of flooding, as has proved to be the case several times, not least in 1960. But the worst floods occurred on 12 October 2000 when the River Ouse burst its banks and the town became an estuary. All low-lying areas of the town were affected, along with more than 800 business and residential properties. A total of 600 homes were evacuated.

Cars were submerged, barrels of beer from Harvey's Brewery floated off down the river, inflatable dinghies conveyed residents through streets where the day before people had walked and vehicles had driven, and firefighters had to fight their way into some people's homes. Ruined belongings appeared in piles and walls collapsed. An ambulance put out a call to a police car as the latter approached in Orchard Road: 'We're floating mate, we're floating.' (The floating ambulance had a life far beyond Lewes when a photograph of it was used on a poster by the World Wildlife Fund to highlight the dangers of climate change.)

In Malling alone, hundreds of people were looked after each day at the community centre. Within a week Lewes had returned to its bustling, if still injured, self. In Malling it took three years for the last person to be rehoused.

It is officially estimated that 2,632 homes remain at flood risk in the Lewes area, 594 of which are said to be at significant risk.

Bibliography

In researching this book I have read or consulted the books listed below. The ever-reliable, indeed indispensable, *Oxford Dictionary of National Biography* has been invaluable in much of the research.

Arscott, David, *Our Lewes* (Stroud: Sutton Publishing, 2004).

Arscott, David, *Brighton: A Very Peculiar History* (Brighton: Salariya Book Company, 2009).

Brent, Colin, *Historic Lewes and Its Buildings* (Lewes: Lewes Town Council, 1995 [revised edition]).

Brent, Colin, Deborah Gage and Paul Myles, *Tom Paine in Lewes 1768-1774* (Lewes: PM Trading, 2009).

Cairns, Bob, *Lewes Through Time* (Stroud: Amberley Publishing, 2012)

Cairns, Bob, *Lewes. The Postcard Collection* (Stroud: Amberley Publishing, 2015)

Clark, Kim, *The Twittens. The Saxon and Norman Lanes of Lewes* (Lewes: Pomegranate Press, no date).

Cobb, Ruth, *Travellers to the Town* (London: Epworth Press, 1953).

Coogan, Tim Pat, *De Valera: Long Fellow, Long Shadow* (London: Arrow, 1995)

Crowther, Annie, *The Public Subscription Windmill and the Round House at Lewes* (Lewes: Piper Passage Books, 2001).

Drummond, John, *Tainted by Experience: A Life in the Arts* (London: Faber and Faber, 2000).

Dudeney, Henry Mrs, *A Lewes Diary 1916-1944,* ed. by Diana Crook (Leyburn: Tartarus Press, 1998).

Etherington, Jim, *Lewes Bonfire Night* (Seaford: SB Publications, 1993).

Fanning. R, *Eamon de Valera: A Will to Power* (London: Faber & Faber, 2015).

Fleming, Barbara, *Lewes: Two Thousand Years of History* (Seaford: SB Publications, 1994).

Goring, Jeremy, *Burn Holy Fire: Religion in Lewes since the Reformation* (Cambridge: Lutterworth Press, 2003).

Ladipo, Sue, *A History of St Michael the Archangel. The Parish Church of South Malling* (South Malling: St Michael the Archangel, 2000 [revised 2002]).

Lucie-Smith, Edward, *Sussex Writers and Artists* (Lewes: Snake River Press, 2007).

Malcomson, R.M., *Daisy Ashford. Her Life* (London: Chatto & Windus/Hogarth Press, 1984).

Martin, David and Clubb, Jane, *An Archeological Interpretative Survey of Bull House, 92 High Street, Lewes* (Lewes: Sussex Archeological Society [Centre for Applied Archaeology, University College London] 2009).

McCarthy, Fiona, *Eric Gill* (London: Faber and Faber, 1989).

Millar, Ronald, *The Piltdown Men* (London: Gollancz, 1972).

Page, William (editor), *The Victoria History of the County of Sussex. Volume Two* (London: Archibald Constable and Company, 1907).

Pugh, Brian, *Bonfire Night in Lewes* (London: MX Publishing, 2011).

Philpot, Terry, *Beside the Seaside. Brighton's Places and Its People* (Hove: Step Beach Press, 2015).

Poole, Helen, *The Little Book of Sussex* (Seaford: SB Publications, 2001).

Rothenstein, William, *Men and Memories* (London: Macmillan and Company 1932).

Salzman, L. F., (ed) *The Borough of Lewes: Introduction and History*, in *A History of the County of Sussex: Volume 7, the Rape of Lewes* (London: 1940).

Shelley, Henry C., *John Harvard and His Times* (London: Smith, Elder & Co, 1907).

Skidelsky, Robert, *John Maynard Keynes. Volume One: Hopes Betrayed 1883-1920* (London: Macmillan, 1983).

Skidelsky, Robert, *John Maynard Keynes. Volume Two: The Economist as Saviour 1920-1937* (London: Macmillan, 1992).

Skidelsky, Robert, *John Maynard Keynes. Volume Three: Fighting for Britain 1937-1946* (London: Macmillan, 2000).

Sox, David, *Bachelors of Art: Edward Perry Warren & the Lewes House Brotherhood* (London, Fourth Estate, 1991).

Thomas, Andy, *The Lewes Flood* (Seaford: S.B. Publications, 2001).

Williamson, Audrey, *Thomas Paine. His Life, Work and Times* (London: George Allen & Unwin, 1973).

Winston, Richard, *Becket* (London: Constable, 1967).

Wilson, Jean Moorcroft, *Virginia Woolf's London. A Guide to Bloomsbury and Beyond* (London: Tauris Peake Paperback, 2000).

Woolf, Virginia, *The Question of Things Happening. The Letters of Virginia Woolf. Volume 11: 1912-1922*, edited by Nigel Nicolson (London: The Hogarth Press, 1976).

Virginia Woolf, *The Diary of Virginia Woolf. Volume 1: 1915-1919*, edited by Anne Olivier Bell (London: The Hogarth Press, 1977).

Young, Bill, in association with Bob Cairns, *Lewes Then and Now* (Seaford: SB Publications, 1998).

Zinn, Howard, *A People's History of the United States* (London: Harper Perennial Modern Classic, 2005).

Acknowledgements

As always, the staff of the British Library were ever-helpful and efficient. Various other people have helped me with this book and I would like especially to thank the following:

Sean Arnold, front of house officer, Sussex Past (Sussex Archeological Association), drew my attention to the excellent leaflet *Tom Paine at Bull House*, by his colleague Mary Burke. The Revd Dick Field of St John-sub-Castro speculated on the likely siting of Prince Magnus's cell, which I have adopted. David Hitchin, author of *Quakers in Lewes: An Informal History*, offered information about the founding of the present meeting house.

Paul Lantsbury, on a memorably pleasant afternoon touring the town, kindly took the photographs attributed to him. Emma O'Connor, museums officer, Sussex Past, enlightened me on several matters. David Parry, senior customer service assistant, Parks and Cemeteries, Lewes District Council, helped me to locate the graves of Wynne Edwin Baxter and Alice Dudeney in Lewes Cemetery. John Russell, honorary treasurer and trustee of the Westgate Chapel (Lewes) Trust, kindly clarified points about the chapel's history and plans for its present restoration. Last but not least, Alan Murphy, commissioning editor at Amberley Publishing, who came up with the idea for a book in their *Secret* series.